7241

"By asking the right questions, Phil Johnson brilliantly exposes
the fault lines of the reigning Darwinian orthodoxy
and challenges its disciples who preach
philosophical naturalism under the guise of science.
The *Wedge* is a must read. Witty, engaging and insightful,
it cuts to the heart of the most crucial issue of our day."

CHARLES COLSON

The WEDGE of TRUTH

Splitting the Foundations of Naturalism

PHILLIP E. JOHNSON

InterVarsity Press
Downers Grove, Illinois

InterVarsity Press
P.O. Box 1400, Downers Grove, IL 60515
World Wide Web: www.ivpress.com
E-mail: mail@ivpress.com

InterVarsity Press® is the book-publishing division of InterVarsity Christian Fellowship/USA®, a student movement active on campus at hundreds of universities, colleges and schools of nursing in the United States of America, and a member movement of the International Fellowship of Evangelical Students. For information about local and regional activities, write Public Relations Dept., InterVarsity Christian Fellowship/USA, 6400 Schroeder Rd., P.O. Box 7895, Madison, WI 53707-7895.

All Scripture quotations, unless otherwise indicated, are taken from the Holy Bible, New International Version®. NIV®. Copyright ©1973, 1978, 1984 by International Bible Society. Used by permission of Zondervan Publishing House. All rights reserved.

Cover illustration: © Hiroshi Sakuramoto/Photonica

ISBN 0-8308-2395-6

Printed in the United States of America ∞

Library of Congress Cataloging-in-Publication Data

Johnson, Phillip E., 1940-
   The wedge of truth: splitting the foundations of naturalism/Phillip E. Johnson.
    p. cm.
   Includes bibliographical references.
   ISBN 0-8308-2267-4 (cloth: alk. paper)
   ISBN 0-8308-2395-6 (pbk: alk. paper)
    1. Naturalism. 2. Apologetics. 3. United States—Religion—1960- 4. United States—Church history—20th century. [1. Religion and science.] I. Title.
   BT1220.J57 2000
   261.5—dc21

                                       00-039586

P	20	19	18	17	16	15	14	13	12	11	10	9	8	7	6	5	4	3	2	1
Y	16	15	14	13	12	11	10	09	08	07	06	05	04	03	02					

To the congregation of First Presbyterian Church of Berkeley, California

Contents

Foreword

As you read this book, you must not lose sight of what is really at issue: the authority of a certain intellectual and moral *style* that characterizes what is "acceptable" or "good work" in Western academic institutions and professional organizations. Does that style have the right to dictate substantive conclusions about reality and the life of reason?

Reason is the human ability to determine what is real or not real by *thinking*. Just as, centuries ago, the honest thinker had to be willing to follow the inquiry even if it led to a godless universe, so today the honest thinker has to be willing to follow the inquiry even if it leads to a God-governed universe. This latter possibility today causes those who think they are in charge of what is only reasonable and right to become impatient and imperious. They cannot afford to be wrong about the godlessness of reality, for now our whole system of education is based on that assumption, just as some while ago it was based on the assumption of God.

And so, as Phillip Johnson so beautifully explains and illustrates, reason is replaced by rationalization. Rationalization is the use of reasoning to make sure that one comes out at the right place. Not long ago the dominant ideal within intellectual circles was to judge the conclusion by the method through which it was derived. If the method was good, you were required to accept the conclusion, at least provisionally. Now, sadly, the method is judged by whether it brings you out at the "right" conclusion, as determined by institutional consensus congealed around glittering personalities. If you don't come to the "right" conclusion, your method is wrong, and you are probably a bad person. Derisive terminology will be used to describe you.

This is of course very old stuff in human history, but it is always difficult to recognize it for what it is. Contemporary certainties never look like rationalizations, or they would not be contemporary certainties. The character of rationalization is hidden beneath the cloak of benign authority.

In our case today, the authority is science. *Science*, we are told, says this or that. We had better believe it. Unfortunately, science says nothing. It is not the kind of thing that can say anything. Only scientists say things, and scientists can be remarkably unscientific and are often remarkably wrong—as subsequent events frequently show. In addition, many who would speak for science are not scientists or have no qualifications in the area of their claims. But if they can assume an aura of "the scientific" in some way, they will be able to rationalize at will and gain a hearing for it.

Phillip Johnson is relentlessly logical. That is, he insists that there be good, or at least some, evidence to support a claim—evidence other than that the claim is of the "right" sort. This is an irritating trait, and plenty of people are irritated by his insistence on evidence. But the insistence on evidence is what from antiquity has characterized scientific work—not a set of conclusions which must be defended at all costs. It is evidence that drives the Wedge of truth.

In American culture today the real issue is who shall have the right to determine policy. Knowledge confers the right to act and to lead. So the question becomes, Who gets to say what knowledge is? If you can successfully define knowledge in such a way that your convictions are knowledge and those of others are not, you get to determine policy, to direct human life.

But if you successfully define knowledge in terms of materialistic "science," then there will be no knowledge to guide life, for "science" materialistically interpreted tells you nothing about how life should be lived. It can help you only if you already know how life should be lived. Which is exactly what naturalism inconsistently assumes, for *its* answers concerning how life should be lived—and it certainly has them—cannot be derived from the science which it proclaims to be the source of all knowledge. It is thus forced into rationalization rather than reasoning. It has, as an intellectual outlook, only a style and no substance.

As you read this book, look to the evidence and breathe the fresh intellectual air that nourishes genuinely opened minds.

Dallas Willard

Introduction

Imagine that you are driving down a narrow road with a cliff on one side and a precipice on the other, when you find that a huge, thick log blocks the way forward. The log is too heavy to lift, and there is no way around it. If you are going to proceed, you must find some way to split the log into segments, so you can move the barrier out of the way. Fortunately, this can be done. The log seems solid, but there are bound to be cracks, some of which penetrate deep into the interior. What you need to do is insert the thin edge of a wedge into the most profound crack and gradually drive the broader parts of the wedge into the log until the crack widens and the log is split.

The log in this metaphor is the ruling philosophy of modern culture, a philosophy called naturalism or materialism or physicalism or simply *modernism*. Under any of those names this philosophy assumes that in the beginning were the fundamental particles that compose matter, energy and the impersonal laws of physics. To put it negatively, there was no personal God who created the cosmos and governs it as an act of free will. If God exists at all, he acts only through inviolable laws of nature and adds nothing to them. In consequence, all the creating had to be done by the laws and the particles, which is to say by some combination of random chance and lawlike regularity. It is by building on that philosophical assumption that modernist scientists conclude that all plants and animals are the products of an undirected and purposeless evolutionary process—

and that humankind is just another animal species, not created uniquely in the image of God.

This philosophy controls academic work not only in science but in all fields, including law, literature and psychology. It is promulgated throughout the educational system and the mainstream media, and government backs it. Superficially it seems as immovable as that great log that bars your progress on that mountain road. But on closer examination, the log is marked by cracks. The most important crack in the modernist log is the difference between two distinct definitions of science. On the one hand, modernists say that science is impartial fact-finding, the objective and unprejudiced weighing of evidence. Science in that sense relies on careful observations, calculations, and above all, repeatable experiments. That kind of objective science is what makes technology possible, and where it can be employed it is indeed the most reliable way of determining the facts. On the other hand, modernists also identify science with naturalistic philosophy. In that case science is committed to finding and endorsing naturalistic explanations for every phenomenon—*regardless of the facts*. That kind of science is not free of prejudice. On the contrary, it is *defined* by a prejudice. The prejudice is that all phenomena can ultimately be explained in terms of purely natural causes, which is to say unintelligent causes.

The Wedge of my title is an informal movement of like-minded thinkers in which I have taken a leading role. Our strategy is to drive the thin edge of our Wedge into the cracks in the log of naturalism by bringing long-neglected questions to the surface and introducing them into public debate. Of course the initial penetration is not the whole story, because the Wedge can split the log only if it thickens as it penetrates. If we are raising the right questions after a long period in which those questions were suppressed, then new avenues of inquiry should be suggested, and thinking will go off in new directions. A new body of research and scholarship will gradually emerge, and in time the adherents of the old dogma will be left behind, unable to comprehend the questions that have suddenly become too important to ignore.

The first steps in the thickening of the Wedge deal with its core proposition that intelligence is a real phenomenon which cannot be reduced to material causes and which can be identified scientifically. The biochemist Michael Behe has described the irreducible complexity of organisms at the molecular level and explained why the neo-Darwinian mechanism of random mutation and natural selection does not produce irreducibly complex adaptations. William Dembski has taken our intuitions about intelligent design and formulated them rigorously both in philosophical and mathematical terms.* Works in progress will explain how Darwinist prejudice has distorted scientific evidence from the fossil record, embryonic development, origin of life studies, and genetics. Other work that is just beginning to take shape will sketch an agenda for research and writing in subjects like history, where Enlightenment rationalist triumphalism has long defined the problems and prescribed the conclusions. The path-setting thinkers of the twenty-first century will not merely build on the twentieth century's accomplishments; they will set off in new directions that will require reconsideration of much that we have taken for granted. It will be an exciting century—and probably a dangerous one.

This book is not about the thicker parts of the Wedge, although I will describe some of them. The scientists and scholars who are

---

*In particular, readers who want to understand the Wedge as a whole should read William Dembski's book *Intelligent Design: The Bridge Between Science & Theology* (Downers Grove, Ill.: InterVarsity Press, 1999), and the essays he has collected in *Mere Creation* (Downers Grove, Ill.: InterVarsity Press, 1998). Another particularly helpful resource is the special double issue of *Touchstone* magazine (July-August 1999) devoted to the intelligent design movement, which may be ordered from the *Touchstone* Web site at <www.fsj.org>

doing that work should have the opportunity to speak for themselves, and so I will write of what is coming only briefly, leaving the reader to go on for further details to the books and collections as they become available. My own continuing work is with the thin edge, which continues to burrow into the log as the thicker parts open up the crack. I want to explain the basic thinking behind the Wedge strategy to the public—especially the Christian public. In particular, it is time to set out more fully how the Wedge program fits into the specific Christian gospel (as distinguished from a generic theism), and how and where questions of biblical authority enter the picture. As Christians develop a more thorough understanding of these questions, they will begin to see more clearly how ordinary people—specifically, people who are not scientists or professional scholars—can more effectively engage the secular world on behalf of the gospel. People are continually asking me, "What is going on and what can we do to help?" This book is an answer to that question.

At the outset there is one thing above all others that readers (whether Christian or not) need to understand. In my mind the most important thing is to get people to ask the right questions, not to try to tell them how to *answer* the questions. In a sense, all who are willing to address the right questions are participants in our program regardless of what answers they want to give. For example, any person who is willing to focus on the problem of genetic information, to understand what it is and how it may be created, is on the right track whether or not he or she is ready to give up on the prospect of a naturalistic solution to the problem. Dogmatism thrives by obfuscation, especially by giving the impression that the really important questions should not be asked. When those questions are clearly placed in public view, the truth has a chance to speak for itself.

This basis defines the Wedge as an intellectual movement, not a confessional movement with an official creed or statement of faith. At the beginning stage, the right question has been whether science and naturalism are really the same thing, or whether scientific evidence may be moving away from the materialist answers. If someone thinks that this is a good question which deserves fair-minded investigation, he or she is traveling side-by-side with us—even if he or she thinks that naturalistic science will eventually solve its problems and provide answers that will even more thoroughly discredit the claim that God took an active role in creation. The naysayers are not our enemy. On the contrary, they are an essential part of the dialogue, to help us make sure that we are testing our own ideas as we should. If we in the Wedge have an enemy, it is not those in open and honest opposition to our proposals but rather the obfuscators—those who resist any clear definition of terms or issues, who insist that the ruling scientific organizations be obeyed without question and who are content to paper over logical contradictions with superficial compromises.

This emphasis on finding the right questions will continue, and so the Wedge will continue to pursue a broad-based program that welcomes the participation of persons who disagree with each other over many details. What will change are the questions, for the first question we are asking will not be the last one. That metaphorical log is merely one obstacle, and in getting past it we will not have arrived at our destination but will have simply made it possible to continue the journey.

Already a new kind of question has surfaced, and a major purpose of this book is to address it. Suppose the critics of Darwinism and materialism are right. Suppose there is no macroevolutionary mechanism capable of generating the new genetic information required for biological creation. How could the vast scientific enterprise, dedicated by definition to the pursuit of truth, have been so thoroughly misled on a point of such immense importance? It may seem impossible that not only scientists but also philosophers and other scholars could have overlooked for so long the contradictions and evidentiary difficulties that are so apparent once they are brought into the light. It is not at all impossible, and when we recognize what has happened we will be led to a deeper understanding of human nature and of the fundamental problems of the human condition.

I'll start that process of understanding by telling the true story of a man who lost his faith at Harvard in the 1920s.

1

PHILIP WENTWORTH GOES TO HARVARD

How Can We Tell Reason from Rationalization?

A Christian Goes to Harvard

In 1932 the *Atlantic Monthly* published Philip Wentworth's essay "What College Did to My Religion." Wentworth had entered Harvard College in 1924, where I became a freshman over thirty years later, in 1957. We both encountered an institution that had long ago abandoned its origins as a seminary for Christian ministers and was pursuing its current naturalistic faith with at least as much confidence as the seventeenth-century Puritans had once had in the providence of God. Wentworth says he came to Harvard with a strong Christian faith, which was then (to his surprise) undermined by the education he received there. We shall see whether that is the whole truth, or whether there is reason to believe that Wentworth was effectively converted to the Harvard faith before he ever left home. As for me, I had turned to modernist thinking in junior high school, just about the time I finished the confirmation class at my local church. I chose to go to Harvard for much the same reasons that an ambitious Roman Catholic seminarian might choose to study in Rome. It was the very fountainhead of the faith I meant to practice.

Whatever differences there may have been between Philip Wentworth and myself, they are small in comparison to the qualities and experiences we shared. While at Harvard we both encountered what Wentworth calls "the intellectual chemistry which has produced this wholesale apostasy of the younger generation." Of course that chemistry had produced the same apostasy for many generations before Wentworth's time and for many thereafter. So when I tell Wentworth's story (which you can read in its entirety at the *Atlantic Monthly* Web site),* I am telling you a story that is representative of the experience of an entire culture of educated people over more than a century.

God the Father

Wentworth grew up in a small city in the Midwest of the United States (as I also did) in a community where his father was a ruling elder in the local Presbyterian church, and the senior Presbyterian minister was the acknowledged moral leader of the community. His earliest memory is of his father leading family prayers after dinner, "giving thanks to God for all the good things we had enjoyed." Indeed, young Wentworth hardly seems to have distinguished between his father and God, who was "merely the head of the world as my father was head of the household." There was no room in this benevolent picture for the cross of Jesus, and accordingly Wentworth never mentions even the name of Jesus, much less the radical teaching in, say, the Sermon on the Mount, still less the agony at Gethsemane and on the cross. This is no accidental omission,

---

*<www.theatlantic.com/issues/95nov/warring/whatcoll.htm>. All quotations in this chapter are from this article.

because the theology of the Wentworth family taught that salvation is earned by following prescribed rules, with no mention of any need for atoning grace. Wentworth describes God as a sort of laboratory scientist in the sky providing rewards and punishments to enforce a purely legalistic morality:

> The world was created by God as a laboratory for testing human beings. In the Bible he had revealed his commandments, which were distinct, direct, and admitted of no argument. Obedience to these instructions was virtue, disobedience sin. The one meant honor and happiness and life everlasting; the other was the way to shame and disgrace in this world, and led to torments in the world to come.

At any rate, that is what Wentworth says he was taught to believe. But did Wentworth's childhood mentor, the Presbyterian minister whom he describes as "a living monument to all the Christian virtues . . . whose never-failing kindness and charity made him universally beloved," actually teach this caricature of the Christian faith? The optimistic religion of the time often did teach that following the maxim "What would Jesus do?" is the path to worldly success. Jaroslav Pelikan tells us that "one of the most widely read books ever written in the English language, Charles Monroe Sheldon's *In His Steps*, first published in 1896, was an idealized description of the success in business and in society that awaited an American community in which everyone decided to follow seriously in the steps of Jesus."[1] It is likely that this book was read and respected in the Wentworth home.

On the other hand, there are signs that Wentworth's description may also owe a great deal to what he learned subsequently at Harvard. The doctrine that God is merely an idealized projection of our human fathers is a central teaching of Freud, who took it from a nineteenth-century philosopher named Feuerbach. Feuerbach also influenced Karl Marx's view of religion, and the ideas of Freud and Marx were setting the intellectual fashion at the time Wentworth was writing. The view that "religion" is primarily a matter of enforcing conventional morality by threats of eternal punishment on the one hand, and promises of pie in the sky on the other, remains a staple of secular rationalist thinking even now that Freud and Marx are in eclipse. The pseudoscience of behaviorism, which was also in vogue in Wentworth's day, teaches that behavior is conditioned by a system of rewards and punishments. I remember how effortlessly I picked up these same fashionable ideas as a college student and how they became the filters through which I interpreted the little I could remember of what my earlier teachers—especially my Sunday school teachers—had said. My selective and distorted memory very likely did those teachers a great injustice. So Wentworth's memory of what he was taught as a child may have a basis in fact, but we might hear a different account from his minister if he could speak to us.

God the Wonder Worker

A second major element in Wentworth's childhood theology was that the way to get what you want is to pray for it. Prayer was a means not for conforming our wills to God's will, but for obtaining God's assistance in our own projects. "It would hardly be possible to exaggerate the importance of a wonder-working God in this Christian scheme of things which I took for granted with the air I breathed," he writes. The wonder-working was not merely theoretical but a part of everyday experience. "Did not our pastor often intercede for the recovery of the sick, and did they not usually get well? Did he not pray every Sunday that the President of the United States would be given wisdom to lead the affairs of the nation, and was not our prosperity the manifest answer?" Wentworth admits that these may seem like childish ideas, but "the child got them from his parents, who shared them item by item with the neighbors, who held the same beliefs in common with one hundred million other people in all the Middletowns of America." Very likely the intellectually sophisticated members of big-city liberal churches would disavow the wonder-working, but such people, "if they go to church at all, tend to do it as a matter of form and fashion; they are moved by no strong convictions." Real religion, Wentworth thought, was to be found among those who are less educated and therefore more credulous.

> To find the original God of Christianity still resplendent in all His glory, still hurling His thunderbolts and making no concessions to rationalism, one should go preferably to a Roman Catholic Church— to the shrine, say, of Saint Anne de Beaupre or Our Lady of Lourdes. There one comes into the awful presence of a real God, who heals the sick, gives sight to the blind, makes the crippled walk, rewards the just, damns the wicked, and in all the vicissitudes of life is able to give tangible evidence of His power in answer to prayer. And the same Deity, less colorful, perhaps, but no less real, will be found among the Baptists, the Lutherans, the Methodists, the Congregationalists, the Presbyterians, and every other sect of Protestantism.

To further illustrate his point, Wentworth quoted a *Chicago Tribune* news story:

> The steeple of the Presbyterian Theological Seminary, at 2330 North Halsted Street, was struck by lightning and set afire. One hundred and seventy-five theological students, residents of a near-by dormitory, rushed into the street in a downpour of rain to help the firemen fight the blaze. Dr. John Timothy Stone, president of the Seminary, heard the crash when the steeple was struck. He rushed out into the storm and called upon the students who were helping to fight the blaze to pray. Dr. Stone and his students knelt on the rain-soaked grass and offered a prayer for the safety of the building. The firemen

were unable to get into the steeple, and by the time they had raised a fire tower and trained a hose on the fire an hour later the rain had put out the blaze.

Wentworth comments that "Dr. Stone's action was entirely consistent with his beliefs as a good Presbyterian. In his moment of danger he did what every religious man or woman does instinctively under similar circumstances: he appealed to the wonder-working God who presides over the Christian universe. And I dare say the good Doctor has already used the incident to point the moral in some stirring sermon."

Here Wentworth's point seems to be that rationalists don't rely on prayer to extinguish fires; they call the fire department. He chooses a curious example to make that point, because the Presbyterians did call the fire department and yet it was the rain that extinguished the blaze. The example is as inappropriate symbolically as it is literally because Presbyterians are at least as famous for working to improve civic institutions as they are for praying. Whether or not his prayers influenced the rain, Dr. Stone's action at least may have prevented the eager students from attempting any foolhardy heroism that could have interfered with the professional firefighters and endangered their own lives. In any case, Dr. Stone's calling was not to save buildings from fires but to teach people how to live. In that calling his methods may have been more useful than those employed by the fire department or by experimental science. Suppose that we were asked to decide not how to extinguish a fire in a seminary building but whether it would be a good or a bad thing if all the seminaries were burned to the ground and their faculties dispersed to do more useful work in secular universities or on collective farms. Would prayer conceivably be useful at such a decision point?

Wentworth never gave a moment's thought to questions like that, as least as far as we can tell from his article, because he seems to have thought only in terms of what philosophers call "efficient causes" as opposed to "final causes." To put the same point another way, he was interested in how to choose the most effective means to get whatever it is you happen to want. He was uninterested—I would even say oblivious—to the far more important question of how we should decide what we ought to want. Accordingly he identified prayer with magic and concluded that the modern world rightly judges science to be more effective than magic:

> I emphasize the importance of this God of magic because He is the source of most of the difficulties with which the churches now find themselves beset. They cannot give Him up and remain Christian; they cannot keep Him and retain the loyalty of educated people. It is a critical dilemma indeed. I was soon to face it in my own life, but at the time of which I write I had no suspicion that it existed.

But did Wentworth really have no suspicion that his childhood faith in a magic-working God would be deeply shaken by what he would learn at Harvard?

Choosing a College

Although Wentworth assures his readers that he had no disposition to disbelieve before he went to Harvard, a different interpretation is invited both by what he says and by what he does not say. Here is his description of his initial decision to study for the Christian ministry:

> I arrived at the age of eighteen comfortably adjusted to the Christian universe in which all things work together for good to them that love God. The example set by my family, and indeed by the entire community in which we lived, convinced me of the truth and justice of the divine plan. As I began to think seriously of what I should do with my life, everything pointed to the ministry as the ideal solution.

Christian living was the way of happiness. And what better use could any man make of his powers than to devote them to the propagation of truth, so that others who had been denied it might be led to share its beneficent effects? The decision hardly called for conscious effort. So in due course I went before the Presbytery of the church, where, to the delight of my parents, I was accepted as a candidate for the ministry. The church to which we belonged published a little quarterly, and the next issue carried my picture with this word of explanation: "Philip E. Wentworth, who came before Presbytery last spring, will start his college work this fall preparatory to entering the Christian ministry."

It is clear already, and will become even clearer as we go on, that Wentworth told his parents and their friends that he would enter the ministry because he knew it would please them, not because he had given any serious thought to whether he had a vocation for that career. The announcement of his candidacy was his goodbye present to his family, delivered at the moment when he proposed to go to a far country to learn from very different teachers. If he had told his father that he was going to Harvard to learn to be an agnostic, there would surely have been trouble. Did Wentworth suspect even then that he would in two or three years be telling his trusting father from a safe distance that he had changed his mind? The saintly minister who had been his mentor understood well enough that his prize pupil was proposing to learn from infidels and that Wentworth was taking no precautions to protect himself from being indoctrinated by their teaching.

Without going into the detailed considerations that influenced my judgment in this matter, suffice it to say that I finally settled upon Harvard. My father was not a college graduate, but he was bent on giving me the advantages of formal education which he had lacked, and he was satisfied to leave the choice to me. But I met unexpected

resistance when I sought the advice of our pastor. He was uneasy
when he learned that I was thinking of going to Harvard. Of course it
was a fine university, but the Unitarians had smirched it. . . . Harvard,
the minister said, had been the Sorbonne of Unitarianism, and I
should run a grave risk of learning false doctrine if I went there.
Instead of flying in the face of Providence, I should do better, he said,
to consider his own college. It was a small institution in Missouri,
founded and supervised by the synod of our church. It had educated
many eminent Presbyterian ministers. I could go there knowing that I
should be safe from all the insidious temptations of rationalism.

He urged me eloquently, but I stood my ground. When I went
before Presbytery I had sworn allegiance to truth and I did not think
it would prove to be as frail a vessel as the good dominie's counsel
implied. I suspected that it might turn out, on closer acquaintance, to
be a little too broad to fit into any narrow creed. I was not primarily
interested in dogma anyhow. Sufficient unto the seminary would be
the evils thereof. First, I would widen my general knowledge. Then,
even if it should be necessary to modify some of my doctrines, I felt
certain that the fundamental verities of religion would remain
impregnable.

So to Harvard I went. On a September evening in 1924, I called to
say good-bye to the old minister, who, throughout his long friendship
with the family, had been almost a second father to me. In the quiet
of his study he knelt beside me and offered up a fervent petition to
God to make me diligent in the pursuit of truth. Dear faithful soul!
Within a year he was dead and was spared the pain of learning that
his parting prayer was being answered—in a sense the irony of which
he could never have understood.

So even before Wentworth went to Harvard he was uninterested
in "dogma"—a pejorative label for the doctrines of his church—and
he was expecting to learn that truth was too broad to fit into the "narrow creed" he had been taught. The words he chooses to describe the

things he would be teaching as a Presbyterian minister are all negative; the words anticipating what he expected to be taught at Harvard are positive. His mentor has become the "good dominie," well-meaning but out of date. Even the reference to the "fundamental verities" of religion sounds ironic following the reference to the "evils" of the seminary, and Wentworth does not tell us what he thought those verities might be, or how they could be distinguished from the doctrines he anticipated modifying. At any rate, he was entirely unconcerned about the risk of becoming indoctrinated in a new faith, probably because he did not see it as a risk but rather as an opportunity. Accordingly, he made no plans to stay in touch with the minister so that this second father could help him to evaluate Harvard's teaching from an independent critical perspective. It appears that he wanted no such restraint on his freedom to embrace the new teaching. That final meeting was a goodbye indeed.

Harvard's Teaching

At Harvard Wentworth unsurprisingly found himself "breathing a wholly different atmosphere." At home he had been taught that the rise of Christianity from the ruins of Rome evidenced the hand of God. His professors denied this. "All events in history were manifestations of cause and effect operating on the natural level." Everything evolved, including God, who began as the fierce tribal deity of a few Semitic nomads and passed through various stages until he finally emerged in the New Testament as the kind father of Wentworth's childhood theology. What Wentworth was taught, in two words, was a philosophy called scientific naturalism. He clearly understood its full implications.

> In the course of time the impact of new knowledge, and especially
> knowledge of science and the scientific method, wrought great havoc
> with my original ideas. All things, it seemed, were subject to the laws

of nature. This concept supplied my mind with a wholly new pattern into which my religious beliefs refused to fit. In such an orderly universe there seemed to be no place for a wonder-working God. He would be an outlaw, unthinkable and impossible. The bottom dropped out of my world, and I wrestled with myself in a futile attempt to patch it up.

Probably the attempt was futile because it was never more than half-hearted and was extremely brief in duration. Could some version of God be preserved by setting him up as the First Cause, the creator of those inviolable laws? No, reasoned Wentworth, because a God who left the world to govern itself by natural law "had hedged Himself about by barriers through which even He could not break." Such a God could not answer prayers, communicate with humans or affect our lives. "Though He might exist, he could be of no service to man." So much for those fundamental verities which Wentworth had so recently described as impregnable.

I studied philosophy and read further about this First Cause. Then I began to marvel at the disingenuousness of the human mind when, unable to imagine how the world began, but demanding some explanation of the inexplicable, it can arbitrarily select three letters from the alphabet and call g-o-d an answer. I preferred to think that we know more about such matters when we admit we know nothing than when we resort to such palpable self-deception.

But was it any less self-deceptive to arbitrarily select three letters from the alphabet and call *l-a-w* an answer? Wentworth went rapidly from skepticism about his father's faith to outright contempt for it, and his skepticism was very selective indeed. There is nothing to indicate that he asked even the most obvious questions about the new teaching that was causing such havoc with his beliefs. For example, why should the scientific study of natural laws rule out the possibility that there are exceptions to those laws? Christians have always taught that natural laws exist, but they have also taught that the laws are subordinate to God and not God to the laws. Joseph knew very well how babies are made, which is why he initially suspected Mary of unchastity, but the authority that made the laws answered his doubts. How could those Harvard professors possibly know that "natural law" is a complete explanation for the existence of the world and everything in it, and that therefore God could only be an outlaw? What experiments had they conducted to confirm this far-reaching hypothesis?

I should remind readers that Wentworth's conversion to naturalism occurred in the mid-1920s, before the triumph of neo-Darwinism supplied a seemingly plausible mechanism for biological evolution and before the Miller-Urey experiment* encouraged chemists to believe that prebiological chemical evolution had an experimental basis. Einstein's relativity was just coming into public consciousness, and big bang cosmology was in the future. Whatever one may think of the situation today, scientific naturalism in the 1920s was transparently a philosophical doctrine that was issuing a lot of promissory notes that scientific investigation might or might not be able to redeem. As far as we can tell from his own account, Wentworth never made the slightest effort to distinguish between what scientific naturalists were claiming and what they could actually prove. And of course he never considered putting the issues before the old minister who had been his boyhood mentor. When a prodigal son wants to follow his appetites, or the latest fashion in idols, he tells himself that he has made a careful evaluation of every-

---

*In the early 1950s Stanley Miller, then a graduate student in the laboratory of Harold Urey at the University of Chicago, obtained small amounts of two amino acids by sending sparks through a mixture of gases thought to resemble the atmosphere of the early earth. The experiment was thought at the time to be a major step toward solving the mystery of life's origin.

thing when he is in reality just going along with the crowd. At such times, the last thing he wants to listen to is wise counsel. If Wentworth had listened to the old minister or to similar counselors whom he might have found even in the environs of Harvard, he would have had to ask his teachers—worse, himself—some hard questions. Instead he swallowed the new teaching whole and apparently without a shred of critical resistance.

Abandoning the Ministry

Wentworth tells us that he never went home during the vacations. He doesn't say why, but a likely explanation is that he had made up his mind early on to repudiate his previous faith and was trying to postpone the inevitable confrontation with his father until he was so far along in his education that there could be no turning back. He did explain something about his changes of thinking bit by bit in letters. At first his parents just encouraged him to pray and read his Bible, but at last they realized that they were dealing not with transient doubts but with a full-fledged apostasy. So in Wentworth's second year his father wrote a letter urging him to leave Harvard, spend some time at home and then finish his education at that small college in Missouri.

> He was now convinced, he said, that my going to Harvard had been a ghastly mistake. Two years of it threatened to destroy the faith which had been instilled into me from birth. If I continued in my present course, he could never forgive himself for failing to heed the advice of our old pastor, who had foreseen exactly what had happened to me. "For what shall it profit a man, if he shall gain the whole world, and lose his own soul?"

This recommendation was presented as advice rather than as an ultimatum, and of course Wentworth gave it not a moment's consideration. Gaining the whole world at the price of an imaginary soul must have seemed a very good bargain indeed. He was already in the process of deciding to become a professor, which was not so much a new decision as a reinterpretation of his earlier decision to become a pastor. As he had told himself before he ever went to Harvard, in choosing to study for the pastorate he had sworn fidelity to truth, not to Presbyterianism, Christianity or even God. Now the Harvard professors had taught him that the truth is modernist philosophy. What better use could anyone make of personal abilities than to devote them to the propagation of truth, so that others who had been denied it might be led to share its beneficent effects? Probably Wentworth would have been embarrassed to convey such blatant sophistry to a man who had taught him from childhood and who would have perceived the self-deception in every word. But the old pastor was dead, replaced by his long-time assistant, and so it fell to the younger man to do the best he could in replying to Wentworth's letter formally resigning his candidacy for the ministry. Wentworth says that "His letter was cordial and tolerant, but it demonstrated so conclusively the impotence of the Church to deal with, or even to understand, the problem of my generation that I shall quote it in full." And so shall I.

April 16, 1927

My Dear Philip,

Your father had frequently talked with me about your difficulties. I was therefore not unprepared for your letter, although the Philip who speaks in these pages is an altogether different Philip from the one who left us less than three years ago.

I need not tell you how sorry I am that you have had to go through this crisis. Most of us, some time or other in our college lives, have had to face the very problems that are yours. If a man thinks at all, such questions are bound to torment him sooner or later. Knowing you as I do, I am sure that you have been honest in facing them. Still, it is the way a man answers that really matters; his doubts may always either make him or break him.

I shall not attempt to debate the points which you have raised. You ought to know already how faith can move such mountains of doubt as the unguided reason may build up. There is only one thought that I should like to place before you. As you have been looking at the fact of Christianity from the point of view of a personal God, have you been absolutely fair in seeking the proof on both sides? By that I mean, have you been reading your Bible, praying, and trying to believe, or have you just taken the external view that it cannot be so, and tried to prove that by your thought and reading? Not one of us could keep his faith in any vital matter if he listened only to those who argue against it. Religion isn't a question of logic or reason, although there is logic in it and a man has to have a reason for the faith that is within him.

However, I am not going to harass you with a sermon. I want you to know that whatever you do and wherever you go I still count you one of my true friends. Whether it means anything to you or not, I am going to pray for God's blessing upon you, that He may lead you out into the fullest life. You are still numbered here as one of ours, and always will be. If at any time I can serve you in any way, you have only to let me know. And be assured of this—that with my hand goes my heart. Yours faithfully, etc.

Wentworth comments that "there is something very touching in the manifest sincerity of such an appeal. But what good is it to urge a man to pray when the whole system of religious conceptions has lost its validity for him?"

On the contrary, I would say that the new pastor's letter was a near masterpiece. He knew from conversations with Wentworth's father and his predecessor that he was dealing with a young man who was puffed up with knowledge. Such a person is reluctant to heed any counsel but his own (I know!), but maybe he will listen to just one crucial point if it is presented dead straight, without any possibility of distraction. The young pastor could see that Wentworth had made no effort to consider both sides of the case and that he had directed none of his skepticism toward the Harvard philosophy, instead reserving all of it for the Christian faith he was discarding. Perhaps he could at least get Wentworth to acknowledge that he had not been fair to both sides, and perhaps that would open a tiny crack in his protective armor that could then be widened. Alas, that reference to prayer pushed the wrong button, allowing Wentworth to pretend to himself that he was being asked to turn to magic to resolve his doubts rather than to search his heart to understand his own motives.

The Aftermath

Wentworth continued on his chosen path, and we hear no more about his father. With each passing year he became more confirmed in his naturalistic philosophy, and yet he seemed more aware of what he had lost than of what he had gained. He saw that Harvard had destroyed his religion without giving him anything comparable to take its place. He doubted that it was on the whole a good thing that other young men were taking the same path as he had done. He realized that a philosophy which deals only with means and not with ends provides no basis for morality.

> The really serious dangers of skepticism become apparent when a student rejects the supernatural part of his religion and concludes that there are no valid reasons left for decent conduct. Robbed of standards, he is likely to adopt the easy ethics of business, which permit a man to do almost anything so long as it leads to success in money-making.

But isn't the student who adopts the easy ethics just following the logic that Wentworth himself had embraced? If one knows only a rationality of means and not of ends, it may seem rational to be sufficiently moral in appearance to avoid getting into trouble, while cutting corners when the opportunity arises to get a lot more of whatever it is you happen to want. What we call "ethics" may be merely a matter of deciding when to take risks and when to play it safe. Wentworth shrank from embracing the consequences of his modernist faith, and yet he still could not imagine that the Christian gospel could have any positive effect beyond providing that stern father in the sky.

> Most men and women are incapable of sustained self-control. Greed, pride, lust, are too much for them. They can be held to the path of duty only by some power outside themselves—some higher authority which is able to generate repressive fears stronger than their native passions. Over vast multitudes the Church has for centuries enforced an external discipline of precisely this kind.

Wentworth says that "they" (*not* "we") can be kept in line only by the kind of religion which generates repressive fears by telling lies. Perhaps the elite who go to the best colleges can afford to recognize these lies for what they are, although it would be better if the common people would continue to believe. And yet it seems that even those colleges may be turning out young barbarians. Wentworth concludes with this rueful paragraph:

> The breakdown of Christianity is particularly unfortunate in America, where our educators are so busy building new dormitories and thinking up new systems of instruction that they do not see how urgently the situation calls upon them to redefine the purposes for which their pedagogical machinery exists. In so far as the colleges destroy religious faith without substituting a vital philosophy to take its place, they are turning loose upon the world young barbarians who have been freed from the discipline of the Church before they

have learned how to discipline themselves. Perhaps this was what one of my least orthodox Harvard professors had in mind when he once said: "There are only a few men in the world who have earned the right not to be Christians."

And so the man who had decided to base his own life on the premise that efficient causes are the only ones worth considering, turned at the end to preaching to others that they had better start figuring out the ultimate purpose for which their pedagogical machinery exists.

The Moral of the Story

I have begun with Philip Wentworth's story because it is paradigmatic of so many modernist intellectuals who thought they were dedicating themselves to a life of reason when, in reality, they were mostly learning to rationalize, to justify what they felt like doing. We all like to believe we are more rational than we really are. The painful truth is that we are naturally inclined to believe what we want to believe, and we may adopt some fashionable intellectual scheme because it allows us to feel superior to other people, especially those unenlightened masses who need the crutch or the discipline of religion. Of course people may also adopt a religious creed in order to justify themselves, especially in times or places where religion is fashionable. Everybody is subject to the temptation to rationalize. The temptation is probably greatest for those with the most intelligence because the more intelligent we are, the easier we will find it to invent convenient rationalizations for what we want to believe and to decorate them with high-sounding claptrap. Unless we take the greatest precautions, we will use our reasoning powers to convince ourselves to believe reassuring lies rather than the uncomfortable truths that reality may be trying to tell us.

I have said that the Wedge is about asking the right questions, and here we reach the first of those right questions. How do we tell reason from rationalization—not just when we talk about others but when we form our own beliefs? How can we tell the truth that makes us free from the philosophical system that keeps us self-satisfied?

Many people think that the best answer is to rely on scientific reasoning, but Wentworth's story indicates two shortcomings of that approach. First, science at best gives us only factual or instrumental knowledge, not knowledge of ultimate purposes.* From science we may learn a great deal about how the world works, and how to get whatever it is that we want, but unless we have another source of knowledge we will have no way to reason about the purpose of life or exactly what it is that a rational person *ought* to want. Just as we have to make certain assumptions about the physical world to do science, we have to make other assumptions about what persons are like to know what they ought to value.

Second, the very fact that science speaks so authoritatively in our culture tempts ideologues and worldview promoters to claim the authority of science as validating claims that in fact are not testable by experiment, and that may go far beyond the available evidence. In a word, the scientific method can be counterfeited, and the counterfeit may be certified as genuine by the most prestigious authorities in our culture. Philip Wentworth's Harvard professors apparently taught him that everything, including God, is subject to natural laws and therefore God is either nonexistent or unimportant. Could this teaching have been a rationalization rather than a truth about the world that the professors ascertained by reason? If Wentworth re-

---

*"Reason is wholly instrumental. It cannot tell us where to go; at best it can tell us how to get there. It is a gun for hire that can be employed in the service of any goals we have, good or bad" (Herbert A. Simon, *Reason in Human Affairs* [Stanford, Calif.: Stanford University Press, 1983]). Simon's remark is quoted as a chapter heading in Donald B. Calne's *Within Reason: Rationality and Human Behavior* (New York: Pantheon, 1999), p. 14. Calne agrees that reasoning is wholly instrumental. It can tell us *how* to get whatever we want but not *why* we should ultimately want one thing rather than another. Of course this is not an inherent quality of reason but rather a consequence of basing reason on naturalism.

ceived an education on biblical principles before he went to Harvard, he should have been aware that the elite (including the churchgoing elite) are particularly skilled at inventing ways to tame God because they desire either to ignore God or to use him for their own purposes. Perhaps he did receive that kind of education and wanted to forget it, or perhaps he was only taught one of those God-taming strategies. Certainly Harvard offered no instruction in how to recognize idolatry.

In the following chapters we will see elements of Wentworth's story enacted on a wide cultural stage. People are always looking for ways to forget God, even if they have to give up reason in order to do it. Idolatrous programs may appear to succeed spectacularly for a while, but in the end they use up their borrowed fuel and succumb to their own inherent contradictions. I believe that this is about to happen to the philosophy that dominated the twentieth century, the philosophy Wentworth learned to take for granted as the way all educated people think. I hope that by the time you finish this book, you will think so also.

Let's go first to see the difficulty scientists are having when they try to account for the origin of biological information within the bounds of a naturalistic philosophy.

2

THE INFORMATION
QUANDARY

*Can Natural Law & Chance
Create Genetic Information?*

A Controversial Interview

Some time during 1998 an Australian creationist organization began circulating a videotape entitled *From a Frog to a Prince,* which aimed to cast doubt on neo-Darwinist explanations of how evolution can take, for example, a sort of amphibian and (given enough time) turn it into a human being. The producers had managed to get an interview with Richard Dawkins, the world's most famous Darwinist, and they gave it top billing in their advertising. What they advertised was not so much what Dawkins said in the interview as what he didn't say. The video showed a narrator asking Dawkins if he could point to any example of a mutation or other evolutionary process that was information-enhancing. (I'll explain what that means presently.) In response to the question Dawkins hesitated for at least eleven seconds, an agonizingly long time in the context of a video interview, before he finally gave a completely irrelevant reply about the transition between fish and amphibians. The creationists were ecstatic. As they saw it, Richard Dawkins—the world's most prominent Darwinist—was so completely flummoxed by their most important question that he had to duck it.

Eventually the tape made its way to Barry Williams, the editor of an Australian journal called *The Skeptic*, who consulted with Dawkins and then published a blistering article with the title "Creationist Deception Exposed."[1] Williams at first seemed to be accusing the filmmakers of altering the tape by substituting a question Dawkins was never asked, but that accusation was never made explicitly and in any case was dropped after the creationists produced the raw tapes. The "deception," if there was any, lay in getting the interview under false pretenses and then using it to embarrass Dawkins by making it seem that he could not answer a fairly simple question. Dawkins explained that on the advice of his American counterpart Stephen Jay Gould, he has a policy of never granting interviews to creationists. He admitted the interviewer and camera operator into his home either because they misled him or because it did not occur to him to ask whether they were creationists. As the interview proceeded, however, he became suspicious.

> The suspicion increased sharply when I was challenged to produce an example of an evolutionary process that increases the information content of the genome. It is a question that nobody except a creationist would ask. A real biologist finds it an easy question to answer (the answer is that natural selection increases the information content of the genome all the time—that is precisely what natural selection means), but, from an evolutionary point of view, it is not an interesting way to put it. It would only be phrased that way by somebody who doubts that evolution happened.[2]

So probably Dawkins, ordinarily as articulate as anyone alive, paused for a long time and answered irrelevantly because he didn't want to give any ammunition to the kind of people who ask for specific examples when Darwinists say they know how genetic information was created. Presumably he was pondering how to get them out of the house with a minimum of fuss. The result was that he gave them more ammunition than they had hoped for by giving the impression that he was baffled by the question and unable to respond.

The controversy over exactly what had happened went on for months, but the disputed details matter very little. Perhaps the creationists misrepresented their purpose, or perhaps Dawkins didn't ask. Even if Dawkins really did have his mind go blank for a time, so what? A moment of confusion could happen to anyone, even a person who ordinarily has all the answers at his fingertips. What matters is not whether Dawkins was tongue-tied on one occasion but why he thought that "only a creationist" would ask for proof that mutations or natural selection create new genetic information, and whether he really can point to concrete examples of information-generating mechanisms that have actually been observed. Dawkins apparently cannot do that, as he demonstrated months later when he published a follow-up paper on the Internet entitled "The Information Challenge."[3] The paper contains much unnecessary background information about information theory, speculates about how a hemoglobin molecule might have evolved from a predecessor through random mutations in inactive genes, and finally explains how it may be possible to infer something about the nature of past environments from the characteristics of modern organisms. All this is interesting in its way, but there is no explanation of how random mutations in genes which are inactive (and hence not subject to natural selection) can be causing massive increases in genetic information.* Above all, there is no description of any mutations which are actually known to have the kind of information-creating power which would be required for creative evolution. The creationists may have to wait for their example not just for eleven seconds, but perhaps for all eternity.

Information theory is a complex subject far beyond the purview of this book, but for present purposes it can be greatly simplified. By *information* I mean a message that conveys meaning, such as a book of instructions. Examples would include the plays of Shakespeare, the local telephone directory, the Windows or Macintosh computer operating systems or a cookbook. All of these examples contain an enormous amount of information. So does the genome of a bacterium, which can be described as a miniature chemical factory of astounding complexity. Some little-understood directing process somehow tells the many proteins in the cell just where to go and what to do when they get there. Dawkins himself likes to say that a bacterial cell contains more information (in the form of programmed instructions) than the entire *Encyclopaedia Britannica.* Our bodies contain a vast number of these cells working together in marvelous harmony. If evolution produced these wonderful things, then evolution must be very productive at creating information. So why would a leading Darwinist think it unreasonable and even reprehensible to ask for a single specific example of an evolutionary process that is known to create information?

Before I answer that question, I need to explain how Darwinists usually describe their subject.

---

*One must always be wary of quibbles when reasoning with Darwinists, who are typically more concerned with protecting their system than with understanding its difficulties. Information can be defined in various ways, and a Darwinist may be able to show that, in some technical sense, information can be slightly increased by mindless copying. What needs to be shown is a process capable of producing something equivalent to a powerful computer operating system or a multivolume encyclopedia.

Evolution as Change and Ancestry

Textbooks typically define evolution not as information-creation but merely as *change*—either "change over time" or "change in gene frequencies."[4] This way of defining the subject makes it possible to characterize any example of change as "evolution." Populations of plants and animals are characterized by genetic variation, and the precise mix is constantly changing as some individuals die and others replace them in the gene pool. Hence there is no question that change (in the sense of genetic variation) occurs all the time, right before our eyes. Neither Dawkins nor any other Darwinist would be flustered in the slightest if he were asked for examples of evolutionary *change*. He would cite (as Darwin did) the breeding of varieties of dogs or other domestic animals, or the varieties of plants produced by expert botanists like Luther Burbank, or perhaps the variations in the size and shape of finch species in the Galápagos Islands, all of which probably descended from a single ancestral type that migrated from the mainland. Scientists have no difficulty providing specific examples of evolution, if evolution merely means change.

Another common example of "evolution" is the change over time seen in the fossil record. According to the geological record, different kinds of organisms have lived on the earth at different times. All these organisms share certain biochemical features. This indicates that they all stem from some common source, which evolutionary biologists assume to be a common ancestor. "Ancestry" is sometimes said to imply no particular mechanism of transformation, but this is misleading. In fact ancestry does imply a specific process, one with which we are familiar from everyday life. Grandparents give birth to parents, who later give birth to children, who still later give birth to grandchildren, and so on until the species eventually becomes extinct.

To say that all living organisms share a common *ancestor* is therefore to imply that evolutionary descent is nothing more than an extension over geological time of the same process of reproduction that we observe in our own lifetimes. The differences between apes and humans—or between humans and bacteria—are thus supposedly an accumulation over millions of generations of the relatively minor changes that might differentiate one ape species from another, or even one individual ape or human from its own immediate parents. If the universal common ancestry thesis is true, then you and I have an ape ancestor, a fish ancestor and even a bacterial ancestor—in precisely the same sense that we have human great-grandparents, except of course that there is a far greater number of intermediate generations between those distant ancestors and ourselves. Common ancestry is typically contrasted with what evolutionists take to be the only alternative: special divine creation of each species. Special creation is considered unscientific and hence ineligible for consideration because it necessarily involves a supernatural intervention in nature that is inaccessible to scientific investigation. With special creation disqualified and no other alternative in contemplation, evolutionists consider the mere existence of common features in living organisms to be irrefutable proof that they are all descended from a single universal common ancestor.

Some evolutionists in good standing have challenged this simple model by distinguishing between microevolution (variation within the species) and macroevolution (appearance of new species, new complex organs and new body plans), suggesting that the latter process differs from the former in kind rather than merely in degree. However, the majority opinion (and certainly that of Richard Dawkins) is that there is fundamentally only one process which involves small-scale random variations (or mutations) and their accumulation by natural selection.[5] Possibly some extraordinary processes have occurred from time to time, but they are not thought to be necessary and can be put aside in popular treatments as technical matters to be discussed among professionals. In their view, what the public needs to know is mainly that "evolution has occurred" and that evolution is a purely natural process guided by natural selection but not by God. Scientists may have their professional squabbles over the details, but there is no dispute among them over this fundamental "fact of evolution."

Some Darwinists even go so far as to argue that their theory can be established by logic alone, so that evidence is not really necessary. Richard Dawkins in particular has speculated that if life exists on other planets in distant galaxies, it must have evolved by natural selection. The reason is that with supernatural creation disqualified as "religious," Darwinian evolution is just about the only remotely tenable theory to account for the changes required to make a world of diverse complex organisms. Therefore scientific evidence is not really needed to prove the theory true any more than scientific evidence is needed to prove that two plus two equals four. Amherst College biology professor Paul Ewald explained to a journalist that

> Darwin only had a couple of basic tenets. . . . You have heritable variation, and you've got differences in survival and reproduction among the variants. That's the beauty of it. It has to be true—it's like arithmetic. And if there is life on other planets, natural selection has to be the fundamental organizing principle there, too.[6]

Darwinists rarely go so far as to say that *no* evidence whatsoever is required to establish their theory, but the theory's logical appeal to the materialist mind is so powerful that a few confirming illustrations are sufficient, and all the textbooks and popular books cite the same handful of examples. I have already cited domestic animal breeding and the natural variation observed among the finches of the Galapagos. The most important confirming examples for present purposes are the examples of adaptive mutations, specifically those that enable insects to become resistant to pesticides and bacteria to become resistant to antibiotics. Skeptics may think it is quite a stretch to assume that mutations of that sort are capable of producing the innovations required for creating insects and bacteria in the first place, but Darwinists refute their skepticism by demanding that the skeptics produce an acceptable alternative. Something has to provide the raw material for adaptive evolutionary change, and they argue that mutation is the only candidate. Natural selection is merely nonrandom death, and at most it assures that creatures which have new adaptive features will tend to survive and reproduce. Only mutation can produce the improvements in the first place, and therefore mutation simply must be capable of doing the job.

In a pinch Darwinists could support that conclusion on logic alone, but to make the conclusion scientific *some* evidence that adaptive mutations occur is essential. Only a little is needed, however, because Darwinists are merely looking for confirming examples of what they already know to be true. After all, what else could have happened?

Why Only a Creationist Would Ask
The Australian creationists asked Dawkins to cite a specific example of an information-creating mutation because they had previously interviewed an Israeli scientist named Lee Spetner who has written a book on the problem of increasing information in evolution.[7] Spetner told them that the adaptive mutations cited by Darwinists are not information-creating. When a mutation makes a bacterium resistant to antibiotics, for example, it does so by disabling its capacity to metabolize a certain chemical. There is a net loss of information and of fitness in a general sense, but there is a gain in fitness in specific toxin-filled environments.[8] By analogy, a random change in my

computer's operating program might on some rare occasion improve its performance if it disabled some component that was causing trouble. There could be a gain in effective performance even though there was an overall loss in information content. Similarly, one can sometimes "fix" a sputtering radio by hitting its case if the rough motion happens to reseat a loose wire or open a short circuit. But no one would expect to build a better radio, much less a television set, by accumulating such changes.

It is probable that the interviewers expected Dawkins to answer the information question by citing the standard examples of adaptive mutations, whereupon they could produce Spetner's work and ask Dawkins if he was aware that those mutations are not information-enhancing. That scenario also explains Dawkins' odd reaction. He probably guessed what the interviewers were up to and had to buy time to ponder how to avoid walking into the trap. He knew that only a creationist would ask for proof that Darwinists can actually demonstrate an information-enhancing evolutionary mechanism because any Darwinist (i.e., any scientific materialist) would either define evolution merely as "change" or be content to *assume* that some known evolutionary mechanism provided whatever genetic information was required. What else could have provided it? To a Darwinist like Dawkins, any person who can even contemplate saying "maybe God" is well on the way to becoming a creationist.

Because the main issue from the Darwinian viewpoint is whether "evolution has occurred," Darwinists are enormously impressed by examples of change, which seem trivial to skeptics. The famous textbook examples of variation in the peppered moths of England or in the beaks of finches on the Galápagos Islands involve only back-and-forth variation within a fundamentally stable species. No new features appear, and there is no directional change of any kind.* Nonetheless, these modest examples are continually cited as proof that evolution by natural selection has been observed to occur and therefore that the changes needed to transform a bacterium into a human being can also occur over the course of many millions of years. So when evolution is defined as "change," the scientists at least have some observed examples to cite, even if they are very modest ones. When evolution is defined as "information creation," they have nothing but speculation. Information-creating evolution is not empirical science at all because it has never been observed either in the wild or in the laboratory.

Paul Davies on the Origin of Life
The possibility that the universe is the product of intelligent design encompasses two distinct subjects, one of which is much more controversial than the other. The relatively uncontroversial subject involves the famous "fine-tuning" of the cosmos that is necessary for life to exist at all. There are dozens of mathematical relationships and constants that have to be set just exactly as they are for stars and planets to form, and especially for the chemicals needed for life to come into existence. The theistic explanation for this extraordinary network of coincidences is that a Designer set them all in place at the ultimate beginning. Agnostics prefer to believe that there are an

---

*Teaching About Evolution and the Nature of Science, a guidebook for teachers published by the United States National Academy of Sciences, tells the finch-beak story in truncated form in order to give the misleading impression that it illustrates permanent, directional change. "A particularly interesting example of contemporary evolution involves the 13 species of finches studied by Darwin on the Galapagos Islands, now known as Darwin's finches. A research group led by Peter and Rosemary Grant of Princeton University has shown that a single year of drought on the islands can drive evolutionary changes in the finches. Drought diminishes supplies of easily cracked nuts but permits the survival of plants that produce larger, tougher nuts. Drought thus favors birds with strong, wide beaks that can break these tougher seeds, producing populations of birds with these traits. The Grants have estimated that if droughts occur about once every 10 years on the islands, a new species of finch might arise in only about 200 years." This omits the important fact that the change was cyclical, and the beak size reverted to normal after a flood season.

enormous number of universes, and we necessarily happen to live in the one that happens to be suitable for creatures like ourselves to come into existence. This subject of a designed cosmos has been very thoroughly addressed elsewhere,[9] and I will say no more about it because this is not the kind of design that threatens biological evolution.

Design at the ultimate beginning is (barely) tolerable within the scientific community because it implies only deism and thus confines divine action to the remote past. This means that science can still explain everything that has happened after the first instant of the big bang, and it also means that there is no prospect of a deity like the God of the Bible, who actively intervenes in human history and judges humans for their behavior. Design becomes vastly more threatening to scientific naturalists if it extends to the origin of life and even to the emergence of human beings. A supernatural entity working that far into cosmic history—billions of years after the big bang and right up to our own beginnings—is uncomfortably close. Such a being might be expected to communicate its will to human beings, and that possibility threatens the very roots of naturalistic philosophy.

The mathematical physicist and scientific popularizer Paul Davies very nearly took the dangerous step from the relatively safe kind of design to the threatening kind in his 1998 book *The Fifth Miracle: The Search for the Origin of Life.*[10] The fifth miracle of Davies's title refers to Genesis 1:11—"Let the land produce vegetation." (The first four biblical miracles are the creation of the universe, the creation of light, the creation of the firmament and the creation of dry land.) It is proverbial in the popular-science publishing world that God is good for sales, and several of Davies's books have some religious reference in the title. Commercial requirements alone seem to have dictated that word *miracle* since Davies begins the book by disavowing it. Like other evolutionary scientists, he starts with the presumption that "it is the job of science to solve mysteries without recourse to divine intervention." That simple *a priori* principle settles the matter as far as Davies is concerned. Whatever God may think about the matter, science insists that law and chance did the job.

If the origin of life was not a miracle, Davies does think that it was a very mysterious event. Not long ago he thought that science was close to solving the mystery. But on investigating the subject to write *The Fifth Miracle* he became convinced that "we are missing something fundamental about the whole business." He concluded that a satisfactory theory of the origin of life requires not just more knowledge of the kind we already possess but "some radically new ideas."[11] So what is the fundamental thing that scientists are currently missing, and what kind of radically new ideas does Davies have in mind?

At the middle of the twentieth century, the reigning belief was that life began with an immensely improbable, chance event. This view was dramatically stated in a *Scientific American* article in 1954 by the Harvard biochemist George Wald. Wald conceded that the spontaneous generation of something as complex as a living organism seemed impossible, but he insisted that such statistical miracles are possible and even probable given enough time. He estimated that two billion years were available for chance to do its work, and he argued that "given so much time, the 'impossible' becomes possible, the possible probable, and the probable virtually certain. One has only to wait: time itself performs the miracles."[12]

Wald's view that chance and time are all that is necessary is now out of favor. Today's dominant view is most comprehensively stated in Nobel laureate Christian de Duve's 1995 book *Vital Dust: Life as a Cosmic Imperative.*[13] De Duve argues that life is the product not of chance but of law-driven chemical steps, each one of which must have been highly probable in the right circumstances. This reliance on laws favoring life is a giant step in the direction Davies wants to go, toward the notion that the existence of life was programmed into the cosmos from the beginning and away from the view that the origin of life was a freakish accident unlikely to occur elsewhere. George Wald's position has dropped from sight in part because it has become clearer that even the simplest conceivable life form (still much simpler than any known organism) would have to be so complex that accidental self-assembly would be practically miraculous even in billions of years. (Natural selection can't help until biological reproduction has started, a point to which I will return in a moment.) In addition, the time available for a statistical miracle to occur has been dramatically shrinking. Evidence of life goes back about 3.8 billion years, almost to a time when conditions on the early earth were inhospitable for even the hardiest bacteria. If life was forbiddingly complex from the start and nonetheless evolved in a geological instant, it must have evolved by law-directed chemical steps that would be likely to occur again in similar conditions.

That is why so many scientists, including both de Duve and Davies, are confident that some kind of unicellular life (or evidence of past life) is likely to be found on other planets wherever conditions are sufficiently favorable. Whether there is any similar "cosmic imperative" that would predestine relatively simple organisms to evolve in the direction of human-style intelligence is considered vastly more doubtful. But our own galaxy alone has some 200 billion stars, and if a few million of these have planets bearing life, there are lots of opportunities for Darwinian evolution to bring life to a stage of consciousness and intelligence. Maybe the laws that make primitive life inevitable also make intelligent life sufficiently probable that the universe contains many advanced civilizations.

So far Davies and de Duve are in agreement. They part company over whether existing chemical laws are sufficient to explain the origin of life, or whether something essentially different remains to be discovered. Orthodox prebiological chemists, including de Duve, see the problem as one of conventional chemistry. Once the right chemicals are in place at the right time, the necessary reactions inevitably follow and life emerges. Hence the experiments that seem important to them are ones that show that some of the necessary chemicals (mainly amino acids) could have been synthesized on the early earth, or could have come to this planet on comets or meteorites. They concede that many of the specific steps leading to life remain to be explained, but they are confident that the picture can be filled in eventually on the basis of the known laws of chemistry, supplemented perhaps by chance events that are not forbiddingly unlikely. This confidence is founded not on experimental results but on philosophy. Scientific naturalists believe that chance and law had to do the whole job, because nothing else was available. The proof that law did the job is that it is highly implausible that chance did it; the proof that chance should get the credit is that chemical laws directing the formation of living organisms are unknown and unlikely to exist. If there are only two possibilities, then the negation of one establishes the other.

For Davies, the solution to the riddle of life lies not in just getting the chemicals together but in explaining the origin of the genetic information, which he calls the "software" of the organism. A living cell is a masterpiece of miniaturized complexity. Its complex protein synthesis operations are coordinated by a program or "blueprint" inscribed in the four-letter chemical alphabet of the DNA and then translated into the twenty-letter alphabet of the proteins. The arrangement of these DNA chemical letters (nucleotides, in technical language), like the arrangement of the letters on this page, is not determined by either chance or the laws of chemistry. Chance produces only random disorder, and chemical laws produce the same simple thing over and over again. If the chemistry of DNA controlled the order of the letters there would be no message, or at least no message with any information content higher than the simple order that is present in the chemical laws. There would be no protein synthesis, and no life processes.

The important thing about DNA is not the chemicals but the information in the software, just as the important thing about a computer program or a book is the information content and not the physical medium in which that information is recorded. Davies believes (erroneously, as I will explain) that once the life processes of metabolism and reproduction are under way, natural selection can supply whatever further increases in information are needed. But metabolism and reproduction cannot get started until an enormous amount of complex information is already in existence.

What was the source of the initial information input? Scientific naturalists or materialists assume that this information is an emergent product of chemistry, and that it somehow forms when the right chemical combinations get going from the right combination of chance and law. Davies says, however, that the leap from chemistry to biology requires something in addition to chance and law, because of the fundamentally informational character of life. Law produces the same simple pattern over and over again—highly ordered, repetitive sequences like crystals or snowflakes. Chance produces disordered, unspecified sequences that show no consistent patterns. No combination of chance and law can do the job because the genetic information, like the information in Windows 98 or the Bible, is *both* highly specified *and* random (i.e., not repetitive). These characteristics are essential for any book or program with a high information content and explain why the nucleotide sequences of an organism's DNA necessarily must be independent of any chemical properties that cause the parts of the molecule to bind together. A book whose letters reflected only the chemical properties of ink and paper would contain no information beyond what is already contained in the laws.

The heart of the problem is that physical laws are simple and general, and by their nature they produce the same thing over and over again. Law-governed processes can produce simple repetitive patterns, as in crystals, but they can't produce the complex, specified sequences by which the nucleotides of DNA code for proteins any more than they can produce the sequence of letters on a page of the Bible. Random sequences, on the other hand, are by definition nonpatterned. To say in this context that sequences are random *means* that they are nonrepeating and hence cannot be produced by a formula such as "do X over and over again." A random assortment of letters also contains no significant information unless the sequence is also *specified* by some independent requirement. Again, think of your computer's operating system or the Bible as an example. Only a very small number of highly specific sequences of instructions will give you a working program or an intelligible Bible. Random deviations from this specified sequence will introduce disorder, and the disorder will only get worse if you add recurring patterns of mindless repetitions governed by invariable laws.

In short, meaningful information-bearing sequences require some third force that works against both repetitive order on the one hand and chaotic chance on the other. Mixing the two together just gives us the worst of both worlds. Here is a pastiche of Davies's sentences from his concluding chapter to give a flavor of the kind of third force he has in mind:

A law of nature of the sort we know and love will not create biological information, or indeed any information at all. . . . The whole point of the genetic code, for example, is to *free* life from the shackles of non-random chemical bonding. . . . The key step that was taken on the road to biogenesis was the transition from a state in which molecules slavishly follow mundane chemical pathways, to one in which they organize themselves to follow their own pathways. . . . Once this essential point is grasped, the real problem of biogenesis is clear. Since the heady success of molecular biology, most investigators have sought the secret of life in the physics and chemistry of molecules. But they will look in vain for conventional physics and chemistry to explain life, for this is a classic case of confusing the medium with the message. The secret of life lies, not in its chemical basis, but in the logical and informational rules it exploits. . . . Real progress with the mystery of biogenesis will be made, I believe, not through exotic chemistry, but from something conceptually new.[14]

But exactly what is this "something conceptually new?" Davies admitted that many scientists would think he was describing "a miracle in nature's clothing." He appealed to de Duve himself for protection, saying that

> deterministic thinking, even in the weaker forms of de Duve and [Stuart] Kauffmann, represents a fundamental challenge to the existing scientific paradigm. . . . Although biological determinists strongly deny that there is any actual design, or predetermined goal, involved in their proposals, the idea that the laws of nature may be slanted towards life, while not contradicting the letter of Darwinism, certainly offends its spirit. It slips an element of teleology back into nature, a century and a half after Darwin banished it.[15]

In September 1998 I heard Davies present this thesis at a scientific conference in Italy at which Christian de Duve and I were also participants. I thought Davies had walked right up to the brink of saying that an intelligent agent had participated in the origin of life, and evidently de Duve thought so too. He accosted Davies immediately afterward and continued with probing questions into the evening. De Duve, as remorseless in his logic as he was courteous in his manner, asked Davies if he was implying that information came first, and chemistry only thereafter. Davies answered that he didn't mean that.* So it seemed that Davies was admitting that chemical laws created the information after all. De Duve continued: "You are reviving vitalism and [Aristotelian] final causes!" Again Davies pleaded not guilty. He assured de Duve that he hadn't really meant that the new laws would contradict the existing laws or reintroduce that teleology that Darwin had banned. After a lot more of this de Duve smiled benignly and said, "I must have misunderstood you."

Put to the test, Davies retreated headlong from the revolutionary implications of his own logic. All that visionary talk merely turned out to mean that we don't have all the answers yet, which is exactly what de Duve and all the other orthodox people have been saying all along. Everybody agrees that new knowledge is needed. The question Davies had seemed to be raising was whether we merely need more knowledge about what chance and law can do or whether science needs to recognize some third factor that is beyond chance and law. It seemed as if Davies was trying to have it both ways.

When I asked Davies why he refused to go further, he told me frankly that he was attracted to the idea that there is some rational principle behind the cosmos that steers matter in the direction of evolving into life and intelligence. However, he was very much

---

*But perhaps he did mean exactly that. In his article "Bit Before It?" (*New Scientist,* January 30, 1999, p. 3), Davies wrote that "normally we think of the world as composed of simple, clod-like, material particles, and information as a derived phenomenon attached to special, organised states of matter. But maybe it is the other way around: perhaps the Universe is really a frolic of primal information, and material objects a complex secondary manifestation."

against any idea of a personal God who might interfere with the operation of natural law. In fact, Davies has said in interviews that the book that set him on his career path was Anglican bishop John A. T. Robinson's *Honest to God*. This 1960s manifesto of theological liberalism also inspired such religious reformers as Episcopal bishop John Shelby Spong to attempt to save Christianity by removing its supernatural elements. Davies explained to one reporter that "we have to grow up and give up the notion of the cosmic magician who waves a wand to create atoms and then life. There's no need to invoke anything supernatural in the origins of the universe or of life. I have never liked the idea of divine tinkering; for me it is much more inspiring to believe that a set of mathematical laws can be so clever as to bring all these things into being."[16]

So theological preference was one reason for not bringing a freely acting intelligence into the history of life. Another reason, as evidenced by the dialogue with de Duve, was that Davies was unwilling to risk being labeled as a creationist or vitalist, and that is surely what would have happened to him if he had attributed genetic information to an unevolved (i.e., supernatural) intelligence. It is tolerable for a cosmologist to say that the laws of physics are rooted in some rational principle, at least if he makes clear that he is not talking about a personal God who intervenes in nature. It is quite another thing to say that some information-creating intelligence was involved in the origin of life billions of years after the big bang. Regardless of any disclaimers Davies might make, scientific materialists would see an intelligent force that operates in the history of life as a cosmic magician, and the conventionally religious would see it as the God of the Bible. When I gave my own lecture at the Italian conference, I drew out the implications of Davies's thinking and asked frankly whether the first commitment of science was to impartial investigation of the evidence, or to upholding materialist preferences regardless of the evidence. De Duve sternly reproved me for "attacking science," and lectured me over lunch on the theme that "evolution has occurred."

Natural Selection Is Not an Information Enhancer

Davies also has a scientific justification, albeit a mistaken one, for hesitating to commit himself to the need for a third factor. He believes that evolutionary biologists have proved that, once the life process has somehow been jump-started, the Darwinian mechanism can do all of the rest of the information building. If that is true, then it is reasonable to agree with de Duve that there must be some quasi-Darwinian process operating in the prebiotic environment. Quoting again from *The Fifth Miracle:*

> Can specific randomness be the guaranteed product of a deterministic, mechanical, law-like process, like a primordial soup left to the mercy of familiar laws of physics and chemistry? No it couldn't. . . . If you have found the foregoing argument persuasive, you may be forgiven for concluding that a genome really is a miraculous object. However, most of the problems I have outlined above apply with equal force to the evolution of the genome over time. In this case we have a ready-made solution to the puzzle, called *Darwinism.* Random mutations plus natural selection are one sure-fire way to generate biological information, extending a short random genome over time into a long random genome. Chance in the guise of mutations and law in the guise of selection form just the right combination of randomness and order needed to create "the impossible object." The necessary information comes, as we have seen, from the environment.[17]

That amounts to saying that the law-chance combination can do the job of information creating after all when the package is labeled Darwinism, and that the Darwinian magician can draw the informational rabbit out of the environmental hat when the rabbit never was in the hat in the first place! We are entitled to ask for experimental confirmation of so marvelous a tale, and of course it won't be forthcoming. When I asked Davies about this, his reply gave me the impression that he thinks that natural selection increases genetic information by preserving copies that are made in the reproductive process. I am afraid this misses the point. When two rabbits reproduce there are more rabbits, but there is not any increase in genetic information in the relevant sense. If you need to write out the full text of the encyclopedia and have only page one, you cannot make progress toward your goal by copying page one twenty times.

As we have seen, the standard examples of natural selection in action involve only cyclical variations in fundamentally stable populations; they do not show a population headed in the direction of becoming something fundamentally different. Simply as a matter of logic, it is absurd to describe natural selection as information generating. Natural selection does not actually "select," much less create. The term is nothing more than a misleading metaphor that merely stands for the proposition that early death or sterility is not necessarily random. Some creatures may survive to reproduce because they have some advantageous quality (like the ability to run faster than their peers when pursued by predators), but the quality has to *be there* already before natural selection can favor it. Death doesn't do any creating, whether it is random or not.

In fact biologists believe in the creative power of the mutation-selection mechanism for exactly the same reason that prebiological chemists like de Duve believe that chemical reactions can create genetic information. They are philosophical materialists (at least for scientific purposes) and identify science with that philosophy, so they assume that nothing other than law and chance was available to do all the creating that had to be done. Davies is not exactly a materialist, but he is a deist or pantheist who wants to avoid any hint of an interfering God. So he also has to believe in the existence of a natural information-generating mechanism. If he calls that mechanism natural selection, there is no risk that any materialist will ask for proof. Only a creationist would do that.

The Computer Metaphor

Because an adequate evolutionary mechanism has to have the capability of a software designer, and because the examples of Darwinian processes that have actually been observed are so absurdly inadequate to do the job, Darwinists have tried to turn nature into a computer. Here is how Robert Pennock, an admirer of Dawkins and a nonadmirer of Phillip Johnson, naively describes the trick:

> In *The Blind Watchmaker,* Richard Dawkins beautifully illustrates the power of cumulative selection with an example that considers the probability that a monkey banging at a keyboard would type out a line from Shakespeare at random. The chance of our monkey hitting upon the line "METHINKS IT IS LIKE A WEASEL" from Hamlet is tiny if we require him to get all 28 characters right in a single step. But switch now to a Darwinian monkey who begins with a random string of 28 characters, produces multiple replications of this sequence with some chance of a copying error each time, and then repeats the process starting for the next set of copies with *whichever of the copies is closest to the target sequence* as the original. If he continues in this way, in a surprisingly small number of generations he hits the target.[18]

Of course the "Darwinian monkey" is really a computer that generates random letters and then produces the target text by retaining the correct letters when they appear in the correct places in the sequence, as they are eventually bound to do. Careful readers of *The Blind Watchmaker* will know that Dawkins admits that the computer analogy "is misleading in important ways," and Pennock seeks to disarm criticism by citing the warning.[19] This concession has not prevented Dawkins and followers such as Pennock from misusing the analogy repeatedly to exploit the very feature that is misleading about it: it smuggles intelligence into an argument whose only purpose is to illustrate how a text can be written without intelligence.

The trick is that it is not cumulative selection that writes the target text. Indeed, the very term "target text" gives away the fact that the program is written to guarantee that the "monkey" will reach the goal. The program designer writes "Methinks it is like a weasel" into the computer's memory along with the instructions for retaining the correct letters and discarding the incorrect ones. If the computer program sends up random letters rapidly enough, the "monkey" can write the entire Bible or the Chicago telephone directory in a matter of hours—*provided that a human being has programmed the target text into the computer's memory.* The reference to copying errors and Darwinian mechanisms is a mere sham which serves only to distract attention from the fact that the computer program would require *less* intelligence if it bypassed the random letter generating program and printed the target text directly from its memory. If "evolution" were programmed by a computer which already had the necessary information in its memory, then evolution would be a guided process and hence a slow form of supernatural creation.[20]

In pointing to the problem that evolutionary science has failed to discover an information-generating mechanism, I do not mean to give the impression that other major problems have been solved. In particular, the entire evolutionary scenario as presently understood depends on the assumption that the DNA contains a program for directing the development of an organism in the embryonic process, so that DNA mutations can reprogram the direction of that process and thus produce macroevolutionary change. Experimental evidence with fruit flies and other creatures has not confirmed this assumption, however. What the experiments show is that the mutations either have no effect on the developing embryo, or they have a damaging effect, leading to death or birth defects unless developmental repair mechanisms can fix the damage. I won't develop that argument further for now, because the Wedge is just beginning to publish work on this subject,[21] and it is premature to take up the next question while the scientific community is still refusing to recognize the information quandary. For today it is enough to say that creative evolution can't be produced without employing intelligence. Once that point is recognized we can consider whether creative evolution can be produced even *with* intelligence.

3

THE KANSAS CONTROVERSY

Can Science Be Defended by Authoritarian Methods?

A Media Firestorm

I knew the Kansas story was going to be a big one on Tuesday, August 10, 1999, when the telephone and e-mail messages from reporters began to pile up. On the following day the ten-member Kansas state board of education was scheduled to vote on its new standards for science education. For weeks the board had reportedly been evenly divided over whether to accept a strongly proevolution draft proposed by a twenty-seven-member committee of scientists and educators. The newspapers labeled one faction as creationists, fundamentalists or religious conservatives. Their opponents were consistently called "moderates," a label signifying rationality and tolerance which journalists tend to apply to the side they favor. During the last few days before the crucial vote, one of the moderates had turned out to be sympathetic to the creationist side, and the new six-member majority was revising the committee's draft in a manner certain to displease the scientific community. The media were poised to make a big story out of this latest outbreak of grassroots dissatisfaction with the teaching of evolutionary science.

What the reporters thought was about to happen had been explained the Sunday before the vote in a front-page story in the *Washington Post* by reporter Hanna Rosin, which was reprinted in newspapers around the country.[1] Apparently relying on reports from members of the original drafting committee who were bitterly at odds with the new majority on the board, Rosin wrote that the Kansas board appeared about to "pass a new statewide science curriculum for kindergarten through 12th grade that wipes out virtually all mention of evolution and related concepts: natural selection, common ancestors and the origins of the universe." Rosin said that the new curriculum would not explicitly prohibit the teaching of evolution, "but its exclusion will severely undermine such efforts when they come under attack from students, parents, principals or local school boards in a state where fights over evolution are as commonplace as cornfields. And because all public schools in the state are tested yearly according to the curriculum, teachers will be pressured to follow the new curriculum."

According to Rosin, the pending expulsion of evolution from the curriculum reflected a change in tactics by a persistently aggressive national creationist movement. Blocked by court decisions from inserting biblical creationism into the school curricula, creationists were now publishing books and encouraging high school students to form clubs where they learned to resist what was being taught about evolution in science classes. This activity had been so successful that Rosin began her influential story by quoting a biology teacher who complained that a third of the students in his suburban high school wrote in a final evaluation that they did not believe a thing their teacher had to say about evolution. At the nationwide political level, creationists had induced several state legislatures or school boards to enact measures that required evolution to be taught as theory rather than fact or that attempted in some way to open the curriculum to criticism of evolution. Rosin explained that this partial success rested on a substantial degree of public support among Americans for either creationism or God-guided evolution:

> The movement's recent success may in part be a reflection of the fairly widespread sympathy for some of its basic principles. According to Gallup polls, about 44 percent of Americans believe in a biblical creationist view, that "God created man pretty much in his present form at one time within the last 10,000 years." About 40 percent believe in "theistic evolution," the idea that God oversaw and guided the millions of years of evolution that culminated with humankind. Only one in 10 of those surveyed held a strict, secular evolutionist perspective.*

The creed of the 10 percent is what the science educators have in mind when they teach that "evolution is a fact." In the language of the Gallup poll question, it affirms that "man has developed over millions of years from less advanced forms of life; God had no part

---

*I need to explain the terminology. *Creationist* in newspaper or textbook usage usually refers to young-earth biblical literalists. Confusingly, Darwinists also use the term for anyone who rejects the belief of the 10 percent—that all living things including human beings were produced by an evolutionary process in which God played no part. This is a deliberate rhetorical strategy aimed at giving the impression that only young-earth biblical literalists are at odds with Darwinism. There are many old-earth creationists who accept the geological timetable of billions of years but reject the idea of an unguided evolutionary process that does all the creating that Darwinists claim. The line dividing old-earth creationists from theistic evolutionists is subtle but fundamental. Theistic evolutionists generally accept the entire Darwinian scientific picture, but say that God was invisible and undetectably behind it. For them God's participation is known only by faith and not by anything detectable by scientific investigation. If a theist says that there is *scientific evidence* of God's necessary activity in biology (e.g., in the irreducible complexity of organisms or the specified random complexity of genetic information), he will be classified as a creationist and excluded from evolutionary science because he violates the rule of methodological naturalism. Finally, journalists and science textbooks always compare "evolution" (implicitly a fact) with "creation*ism*" (the "ism" designating an ideology). This is tendentious, since it loads the evaluative scales in favor of the former. There should be an *ism* at the end of both words or neither. Having made this point once, I will accept the usual terminology when others use it without further protest.

in this process." It is not surprising that in a country where the vast majority of citizens believe in God, it is controversial to require that the public schools teach as fact (or as implicit in the very definition of "science") that God played no discernible part in the creation of plants, animals and human beings. It is also not surprising that many citizens, unpersuaded by official reassurances that "science and religion are separate realms,"[2] suspect that a religious or antireligious ideology lies behind the enormous importance science educators attach to persuading young people that evolution is their creator.

Most of Rosin's story gave the impression that the creationists were the aggressors in a programmed nationwide campaign in which Kansas was merely the latest target. One paragraph acknowledged, however, that in reality it was the science educators who were pushing for change on the basis of an organized nationwide campaign:

> The century-old debate erupted again, ironically, in part out of a push to improve science education. About five years ago, a craze for national standards and accountability in every subject swept American classrooms. In response, national groups of science educators wrote benchmarks for scientific literacy to serve as models for states. The idea was to replace blind memorization of facts and figures with broad central concepts. With evolution, the results were not what scientists had predicted. Religious conservatives tapped into skepticism from inside and outside the scientific community to discredit evolution, seizing on routine disagreements among scientists to disparage it as nothing more than a theory.

We can flesh out this picture of local creationists reacting to an initiative from science educators with some facts.[3] What was specifically at issue in Kansas was a proposal from scientists and educators to replace the existing standards, last revised in 1995, with new standards based on a model from national science organizations. The 1995 standards contained only sixty-nine words directly about evolution. The draft proposed by the twenty-seven-member committee devoted almost ten times as many words to the subject and added evolution to the list of basic "unifying concepts and processes" which underlie all areas of science. So evolution was promoted from the status of a theory of biology to that of a fundamental concept of science (ranking it with such other concepts as measurement and evidence). The committee defined *science* as "the human activity of seeking natural explanations for what we observe in the world around us," thus linking scientific investigation explicitly with philosophical naturalism. What the science educators described as "replacing blind memorization of facts and figures with broad central concepts" looked to critics like a campaign to extend scientific authority to questions of religion and worldview about which the public schools are supposed to be neutral. If a central objective of science education is to instill a naturalistic way of thinking, then both the educators and their critics were right.

Extrapolating Macro from Micro

The conservative board members also objected to the eagerness of the science educators to extrapolate grandly from minimal evidence, turning a process that was observed to produce only cyclical variations in fundamentally stable species into a mechanism capable of creating plants and animals in the first place. The science educators' draft observed that "using examples such as Darwin's finches or the peppered moths of Manchester* helps develop understanding of nat-

---

*The Kansas evolutionary biologists were apparently unaware that the classic example of "industrial melanism" in the peppered moths of the English midlands has been discredited. This is not surprising, because American science reporters have been reluctant to publicize this major embarrassment for Darwinists. Supposedly, dark moths predominated when the background

ural selection over time." It defined *macroevolution* merely as "evolution above the species level," and provided no indication that there is a huge difference between mere variation and creation of new types of complex organs or body plans. Feeling that they were being subjected more to a sales pitch for naturalism than to a genuine educational proposal, the board majority in its final product cut down on the emphasis (reducing the proposed 664 words to 392) and distinguished sharply between microevolution (required) and macroevolution (optional for local districts). But the potentially most significant change involved only a single word and was overlooked by the journalists. Whereas the drafting committee had defined science as the human activity of seeking *natural* explanations, the board substituted that "science is the human activity of seeking *logical* explanations for what we observe in the world around us" (emphasis added). If you think there may be a difference in some cases between *natural* explanations and *logical* explanations for certain features of life, then you are well on your way to becoming a creationist. Within the community of evolutionary scientists, naturalism and rationality are considered to be virtually the same thing.

The board's standards regarding evolution then went on to more specific points. Because the revised standards were produced by altering the educators' draft, the wording was awkward in places. These standards were later subject to further rewriting because the national science organizations decided to protest the board's decision by denying it permission to use any copyrighted material. To give a flavor of what was at stake, however, here is a sample with

---

tree trunks were dark (because they were more difficult for predator birds to spot), and light moths predominated in the population when air pollution was removed and the trees became lighter in color. In fact, the population shifts occurred under varying conditions, and the moths do not sit on tree trunks. Textbook photographs were staged by placing torpid moths on the trunks. For details see the article by Jonathan Wells, "Second Thoughts About Peppered Moths," on the Web at <www.arn.org/docs/wells/jw_pepmoth.htm>. Wells describes this and other textbook myths in his book *Icons of Evolution,* to be published by Regnery in late 2000.

the board's amendments in italics:

[8th graders should understand that] (a) Over time, genetic variation acted upon by natural selection has brought variation in populations. This is termed microevolution. A structural characteristic or behavior that helps an organism survive and reproduce in its environment is called an adaptation. When the environment changes and the adaptive characteristics or behaviors are insufficient, the species becomes extinct. (b) Instruction needs to be designed to uncover and prevent misconceptions about natural selection. *Natural selection can maintain or deplete genetic variation but does not add new information to the existing genetic code.* Using examples of microevolution such as Darwin's finches or the peppered moths of Manchester *helps develop understanding of natural selection.* Examining fossil evidence assists the students' understanding of extinction as a natural process that has affected Earth's species. . . . *Understand that natural selection acts only on the existing genetic code and adds no new genetic information.* . . . Selection (natural and artificial) provides the context in which to ask research questions and yields valuable applied answers, especially in agriculture and medicine. [The 12th grade standards add that] the students will understand . . . that biologists recognize that the primary mechanisms of genotypic change are natural selection and random genetic drift. Examples: Natural selection includes the following concepts: 1) Heritable variation exists in every species; 2) some heritable traits are more advantageous to reproduction and/or survival than are others; 3) there is a finite supply of resources available for life; not all progeny survive; 4) individuals with advantageous traits generally survive; 5) the advantageous traits increase in the population through time. [Emphasis added to highlight significant changes.]

As you can see, the widespread reports about the decision (probably influenced by the expectations raised in the *Washington Post* story) were incorrect in stating that the board had virtually

eliminated evolution and natural selection from the curriculum.*
On the contrary, the board greatly improved the intellectual content of the standards on these subjects by encouraging teachers to
raise three important considerations that many science educators
do not want the students to think about: (1) the mechanisms of
*micro*evolution do not necessarily explain how *macro*evolution can
occur, especially when the latter category involves not merely speciation but the creation of new complex organs; (2) natural selection adds no new genetic information to the organism; and (3) a
vast historical scenario like "evolution" necessarily involves a
degree of speculation that is absent from, say, the typical chemistry experiment. When educators say that science teaches that water
is made up of hydrogen and oxygen, they are making a very different kind of statement than when they say that science teaches that
life arose by chemical evolution without the need of assistance
from God. If the educators want to teach the students to think like
good scientists rather than to believe uncritically whatever "science says," then they need to teach the students that sometimes the
authority of "science" is used to validate claims that are based
largely on speculation.

What the reporters had right was the general impression that the
board had drawn a line in the sand over fundamental concepts.
Although the board's action did not forbid local school districts and
teachers from teaching anything, including the customary view that
macroevolution is merely microevolution continued over sufficient
time, it offended the Darwinists by drawing attention to both the
information creation problem and the extrapolation problem. Is the

---

*The board's final version of the standards also omitted any specific reference to the big bang
and suggested that "at least some stratified rocks may have been laid down quickly, such as
Mount Etna in Italy or Mt. St. Helens in Washington State." This lent support to claims that
some board members favored a young-earth version of creationism, but the main issue was
the elimination of macroevolution from the category of required subjects.

"evolution" that biologists observe merely a matter of variation within preexisting species or types, or is it a genuine creative process that over time can produce new complex organs and new kinds of organisms? Can scientists actually confirm the existence of mutations or other natural evolutionary processes that are capable of providing the necessary vast quantities of new genetic information, or is the genetic information possibly the product of a preexisting, creative intelligence (like God)? Those are the questions that the board members wanted to open up for discussion.

The science educators resist not because the questions are unreasonable but because they put the spotlight on the weak points in Darwinian theory. Everyone familiar with the literature knows that there has long been skepticism within the scientific community about the gigantic extrapolation from in-species variation to creative *macro*evolution.* In 1980 the most prominent American Darwinist, Harvard professor Stephen Jay Gould, published an article in a professional journal which took dead aim at the standard textbook claim that "all evolution is due to the accumulation of small genetic changes, guided by natural selection, and that transspecific evolution is nothing but an extrapolation and magnification of the events that take place within populations and species." Gould commented that this theory had "beguiled me with its unifying power when I was a graduate student in the mid-1960's, [but] since then I have been watching it slowly unravel as a universal description of evolution." Gould concluded that if the neo-Darwinian theory means what the textbooks say, "then that theory, as a general proposition, is effec-

---

*Microevolution is often defined as variation within the biological species, and macroevolution as the creation of new species. This way of explaining the distinction is unsatisfactory, however, because (under the most common definition) a species is simply an isolated breeding group. A subpopulation could therefore be called a new species if it lost the ability to breed with the main population, even though it possessed no other new attributes. What a theory of macroevolution needs to explain is not merely reproductive isolation but the appearance of new complex organs, involving an increase in genetic information.

tively dead, despite its persistence as textbook orthodoxy."[4]

Gould came to his skepticism primarily because of his knowledge of fossils. The prominent British developmental biologist Brian Goodwin came to a similar conclusion on the basis of his knowledge of embryology. He wrote that "Darwin's assumption that the tree of life is a consequence of the gradual accumulation of small hereditary differences appears to be without significant support. Some other process is responsible for the emergent properties of life, those distinctive features that separate one group of organisms from another—fishes and amphibians, worms and insects, horsetails and grasses."[5] Lynn Margulis, famed for her theory that mitochondria were once independent bacterial cells, regularly challenges scientific colleagues to name a single unambiguous example of the formation of a new species by the accumulation of micromutations. The challenge being unmet, she commented acidly that science will one day judge neo-Darwinism as "a minor twentieth-century religious sect within the sprawling religious persuasion of Anglo-Saxon biology."[6] I know from experience that such anti-Darwinian sentiments are common among scientists. When I speak to scientific groups and describe macroevolution as the accumulation of small random variations by natural selection, I am frequently charged with inventing a straw man, because "nobody believes that any more." The sophisticated evolutionists are supposedly discovering new mechanisms with names like "autocatalytic sets" and "self-organizing systems" that will replace natural selection—if they can ever find experimental verification. When the same scientists sense that creationists are making trouble, however, they revert to the official story and insist that all reputable scientists agree that evolution is a single process in which fundamentally new things appear by an extension of the same process observed in finch beak variation.

Darwinists tend to be resentful when creationists quote recognized evolutionary authorities as I have just done, as if it were somehow dishonest to quote dedicated believers in "evolution" (however vaguely defined) for a contrary position. No doubt this is what Hanna Rosin had in mind when she wrote that creationists make a practice of "seizing on routine disagreements among scientists to disparage it [evolution] as nothing more than a theory." Admissions of the kind I have quoted amount to something more significant than routine disagreements, however. Persons who suspect that the conclusions and evangelical fervor of Darwinists reflect ideology rather than scientific data have every right to cite contradictions among the Darwinists over basic issues as reason for taking the entire enterprise with a grain of salt.[7] Moreover, there are also writers with impressive academic credentials, such as Wedge members Michael Behe[8] and William Dembski,[9] who are taking this criticism to its logical conclusion. They are pressing the claim that the Darwinian mechanism is inherently incapable of producing the irreducible and specified informational complexity characteristic of living organisms. Their work is controversial, of course, but it is difficult to maintain that there is no controversy worth discussing when books and articles about the controversy are appearing regularly. Darwinists respond that there is no controversy over the "fact of evolution" within the scientific community, but that may be due to the philosophical bias that is enforced within that community rather than to the state of the evidence.

The Press Reaction

The creation-evolution controversy is one of those subjects that has become standardized in the press. I sometimes have the impression that journalists just click on a "bash creationism" macro in their word processors and sit back while the printer pours out a string of clichés: the Catholic Church persecuted Galileo, the Scopes trial in

1925 should have settled this matter, the Bible is not a scientific textbook, scientists agree that "evolution has occurred," mainstream religious leaders say that God and evolution are compatible, and the country will fall into ruin if evolution is not emphasized in the schools. Even the feeble witticisms are standardized, as columnists either exploit the irony that "creationism is evolving" or speculate that the next creationist move will be to declare the earth flat, while the editorial cartoonists caricature opponents of Darwinism as apemen.[10] The journalistic macro learned what little it knows about the subject from polemics by scientific materialists like Isaac Asimov, Carl Sagan, Richard Dawkins and Stephen Jay Gould, who are accepted by journalists as impartial authorities because they speak in the name of "science." So the macro defines creationists as Bible thumpers who either are ignorant of the scientific evidence that contradicts their position or choose to disregard it. From that starting point it is inconceivable that creationists could have any rational arguments to make, and you can cite just about anything you like, from fossils to finch beaks to pesticide resistance, to make them look like people blind to facts. There is no need to try to understand the dissenting point of view because according to the macro all doubts about evolution are irrational *by definition*.

Some columnists seized the opportunity to ridicule a class enemy deemed incapable of fighting back. The *Washington Post*'s Gene Weingarten imagined God sarcastically thanking creationists for their support and then telling them to "go forth and multiply. Beget many children. And yea, your children shall beget children. And their children shall beget children, and their children's children after them. And in time the genes that have made you such pinheads will be eliminated through natural selection. Because that is how it works." How many large social groups can be described as "pinheads" these days and nominated for extinction without the risk of retaliation? The most unrestrained abuse came from England, where journalists like to show off their talent for invective. The prolific author A. N. Wilson, a lapsed Christian who has written critical biographies of Jesus, Paul and C. S. Lewis, condemned the entire American Midwest as the "land of the born-again boneheads." There are some reasonable people in the United States, Wilson conceded, "nearly all of them living on the eastern seaboard and in the big cities." In states such as Kansas, however, "the stupidity and insularity of the people is quite literally boundless. . . . These are the people who believe that Elvis Presley has risen from the dead or that President Clinton has repented of his sins and never looked at another bimbo since Monica." I read that passage aloud to a lecture audience in Kansas City, and they laughed heartily with me at the stupidity and insularity of a London intellectual who thinks that it is characteristic of conservative Midwestern Christians to worship Elvis or to put their faith in the promises of Bill Clinton.

Even the commentators who tried to be polite had difficulty grasping how anyone could refuse to believe facts that farmers as well as scientists observe every day. Jonathan Weiner, author of a prizewinning popular treatment of evolution titled *The Beak of the Finch,* wondered how any farmer could be a creationist when "evolution is happening all the time, literally under our noses."

> Every time a hospital runs into a staph or strep infection that resists antibiotics, it is confronting evolution in action. Every time a farmer sprays pyrethroids and cotton moths go right on eating his cotton, that farmer is confronting evolution in action too. A biologist once told me: "These people are trying to ban the teaching of evolution while their own cotton crops are failing because of evolution. How can you be a creationist farmer any more?[11]

Of course the Kansas board *endorsed* the teaching of pesticide resistance as microevolution, and those farmers (who rarely try to grow cotton in Kansas) are well informed about pesticide resistance and animal breeding. What they doubt is that evidence of cyclical variation within a species illustrates how you get plants and animals in the first place. It seemed that Weiner had never heard of the distinction between *macro-* and *micro*evolution, indicating that he may be a victim of inferior science education. Dr. Maxine Singer, a noted molecular biologist and president of the Carnegie Institution, appeared to be similarly uninformed:

> [Creationists] assert that disputes among scientists regarding the details of evolutionary processes cast doubt on the theory as a whole. But they give themselves away when they dwell on particular aspects of evolution that trouble their beliefs. I saw this recently when I talked with several members of the [Kansas] board. They accepted that within a species individual traits can change continually. But they were unwilling to recognize that some changes can lead to the emergence of new species, as when humans and apes evolved from a common ancestor.[12]

For Maxine Singer and Jonathan Weiner—and for their local counterparts who made impassioned pleas on behalf of evolution at the Kansas board hearings—only blind religious prejudice could explain why anyone could doubt that pesticide resistance and finch-beak variation illustrate a process capable of evolving human beings not only from that hypothetical common ancestor with apes but ultimately from bacteria.

The most poignant example of this widespread inability to credit creationists with even a minimum degree of rationality came from a *Chicago Tribune* story by a staff reporter named Julia Keller.[13] Julia Keller has a brilliant sister named Lisa whose "A" in calculus "only complemented similar academic triumphs in biology and other hard sciences." But Lisa has for some unexplained reason become a Christian and is now "deeply conflicted about issues such as evolution and the Big Bang, scientific theories that seem to contradict the very Scripture that has given her life meaning and purpose." Julia herself is troubled by the contradiction between what her brilliant sister has come to believe and what the infallible authorities of science have taught *her* to believe. When Julia heard about the Kansas decision, "I had a sudden, appalling vision of the lights going out all over Kansas in a steady encroachment of medieval darkness. . . . I can snicker at the creationists and their ostrich-like approach to science. But I can't snicker at my sister. She is a brilliant, well-intentioned and troubled by the apparent contradiction between her head and her heart, between her intellect and her soul."

Julia Keller may not snicker at her sister, but she sure does patronize her. Despite her gushing over Lisa's intelligence—"her nimble mind, her love of the rigors of scientific inquiry"—the possibility never crosses Julia's mind that the Lisa who excelled at hard science might know something about the evidence and have rational doubts about whether it proves everything the Darwinists claim it does. Julia herself merely parrots the words of Stephen Jay Gould as if *they* were Scripture while smugly displaying her compassion for the brilliant sister who is hiding from reality because her beliefs "give her comfort and solace."

Everyone who questions evolutionary naturalism experiences this patronizing contempt, reminiscent of those disciples of Freud who used to tell people who challenged Freud's theories that they were displaying symptoms of "resistance," the cure for which is psychoanalysis. In the *National Post of Canada* Philip Mathias wrote that he had graduated some years back from London University after studying chemistry, physics, mathematics and evolutionary biology. His experience is that "I have tried to debate evolution with many scientists, and their reaction is always the same—at first, the discomfort felt by a believer faced with an unbeliever, and then, when the light dawns, contempt for somebody they believe must be a religious nut."[14] This reaction goes a long way toward explaining why there are so few persons with careers in mainstream science who are willing to challenge Darwinism. It is permissible to dispute questions of detail, but a scientist who challenges the philosophical consensus that supports the theory risks unfavorable peer reviews, which tend to lead to loss of funding and consequent unemployment.

The Political Reaction

The press reaction to the Kansas rebellion was universally strident, with table-pounding editorials and hostile commentary from every major newspaper in the United States as well as many from abroad. The inevitable result of the media firestorm was to bring the issue into the presidential campaign, where the candidates were more concerned with the public opinion polls than with the opinions of journalists. There are a lot of creationists in America, possibly an overwhelming majority if the term is defined broadly enough to include those who believe that God actively guided evolution.* A Gallup poll conducted in late June 1999 revealed that Americans favor teaching creationism in public schools along with evolution by 69 percent to 29 percent. They also oppose by 55 percent to 40 percent replacing evolutionism altogether with creationism, a margin that I am sure the science educators do not find very reassuring.[15]

Given this polling data, it is not surprising that the Republican presidential candidates, especially front-runner George W. Bush, endorsed

---

*The categories are clouded because of persistent confusion over whether God-guided gradual development of life should be classified as evolution or creation. In scientific circles the distinction turns on whether God's guidance is deemed to make any scientific difference. Persons who claim that there is scientific evidence for God's participation are dismissed as creationists; persons who acknowledge that there is no scientific evidence for divine guidance and thus leave God entirely in the realm of subjective faith are tolerated as evolutionists.

local control of the public schools and said that they had no objection if the local board chose to teach both sides of the controversy. What truly shocked the scientific community, however, was the embarrassing series of waffles by Vice President Al Gore, a liberal who (in the sarcastic words of a *Washington Post* editorial) "has held himself out as an avatar of science education."[16] Gore first failed to criticize the Kansas decision, then said he supported the teaching of evolution but also believed localities should be free to teach creationism. He modified this position to say that (in view of constitutional considerations) localities should be free to teach creationism in the context of religion classes but not in science classes; finally he gave in to vehement protests from the scientific community and declared that the Kansas decision was a mistake and that he opposed it.

The University of Kansas Enters the Fray

University of Kansas chancellor Robert Hemenway announced his views about the controversy in a full-page editorial in the October 29, 1999, issue of the *Chronicle of Higher Education*.[17] Hemenway acknowledged that the state board of education had not banned the teaching of evolution, and he thought that most local schools would continue to teach the subject as before. He also predicted that the incumbent religious conservatives would be defeated in the next election, and the board would go back to supporting the teaching of macroevolution. That seems to imply that the whole controversy was overblown,* but Hemenway nonetheless thought he discerned *motives* behind the board's decision which were ominous for both Kansas and the nation as a whole. He wrote that the current board majority

---

*Hemenway may have begun his article with these reassuring comments to head off efforts by some scientists to punish Kansas's students for the board's action. For example, *Scientific American* editor-in-chief John Rennie urged scientists on university admissions committees

wishes to destroy the idea that the public schools should be a source of truth or certainty. Whereas educational institutions—especially colleges and universities—define their mission as the pursuit of truth, the majority of the board seems to believe that the only sources of truth or certainty are the church and the family. According to that view, family values are expressed as the family's right to determine what a child shall believe, and religious values are expressed as theological beliefs that schools must accommodate. If scientific evidence conflicts with those religious beliefs, science must be rejected, no matter the weight of the evidence.

That is a highly exaggerated way of saying that the board members thought that the views of parents should be given some consideration and that as elected representatives they should not restrict themselves to rubber-stamping the dictates of the professional educators. It also begs the question since the board's position was not that religious beliefs should be protected regardless of the evidence but rather that macroevolutionary claims go far beyond the scientific evidence. From that standpoint, it is the science educators who insist that scientific evidence should be rejected if it conflicts with their religious belief in favor of evolutionary naturalism. Hemenway responded that the conservative board members are as far out of step with enlightened opinion on the religious questions as they are on the scientific questions:

The most disturbing part of the board's debate on all of the versions was the clear suggestion from the majority of the board that one could not believe in both God and evolution—or, for that matter, in

to notify the Kansas governor and the state board of education that "in light of the newly lowered education standards in Kansas, the qualifications of any students applying from that state in the future will have to be considered very carefully." Rennie explained that the purpose of these warnings would be to "send a clear message" to the parents in Kansas that this bad decision carries consequences for their children (John Rennie, "A Total Eclipse of Reason," *Scientific American,* October 1999, <www.sciam.com/1999/1099issue/1099commentary.html>).

both God and science. Devout people—including many scientists—who find no conflict between their religion and their beliefs in evolution have been deeply offended by the board's action, feeling that it is an attempt to impose the religious views of the majority of the board on others. The fact that an incompatibility between science and religion has been rejected by Pope John Paul II, most Jewish theologians, and the majority of mainline Protestant denominations seemed not to affect the board's decision.

I'll address the religious questions in the next chapter. For now the important point is that Hemenway made no reference to the primary disputed scientific issues—the extrapolation from micro to macro and the creation of genetic information—in calling for universities to join in "a crusade for science education across the country." Specifically, Hemenway proposed an educational campaign to increase scientific literacy not only among students but also the general public. Science education, he argued, should be broadened to prepare future scientists and teachers to engage in public debates. "Additional courses in rhetoric and argument, political discourse, and the relationship of science and theology might help prepare young scientists and science teachers for a public role." One of the objectives of this public debate would be to correct "the mistaken notion that one must choose between God and science." Another would be to provide "teams of professors available to respond to requests for help whenever a state or local school board debates whether to teach evolution." Chancellor Hemenway then appointed a task force of faculty and administrators at his own university to draft plans for carrying forward this broadened educational program. It seems that their task is to devise a strategy for marginalizing dissent from Darwinism and materialism by making it seem that there are no real issues in dispute, just people who are so misinformed that they don't understand that the ruling authorities have all the right answers.

The editors of the *Chronicle of Higher Education* allowed me to respond to Chancellor Hemenway's manifesto two weeks later.[18] I applauded the idea of educating scientists and citizens to take part in public discourse about evolution, but I cautioned that "educators should aim to educate, and not to indoctrinate or wage a propaganda campaign." That requires that students be exposed not only to orthodox views on the subject but also to dissenting views that are widely held among the public, including the college-educated public. How can students become skilled in public discourse about evolution if they learn only a caricature of the dissenting views and never find out about the evidentiary problems?

What educators in Kansas and elsewhere should be doing is to "teach the controversy." Of course students should learn the orthodox Darwinian theory and the evidence that supports it, but they should also learn why so many are skeptical, and they should hear the skeptical arguments in their strongest form rather than in a caricature intended to make them look as silly as possible. They should also learn that there really is a tension between the idea that a supernatural being called God brought about our existence for a purpose and the contrasting idea that we are products of an unguided and purposeless material process. Why else would persons who want to mock the Christian fish symbol choose to decorate their automobile bumpers with a fish with legs? You can paper over the tension by saying that some scientists are "religious" in some vague sense, but why not face up to the problem and educate people about the various options? Denying the obvious isn't good education, and in the long run it won't build credibility for science.

The "teach the controversy" formula probably has the support of about two-thirds of the American public, and some members of the majority of the Kansas state board of education have endorsed it publicly. With such a genuinely liberal educational approach readily available, the only reason for turning to a propaganda campaign instead must be that the science educators are not confident that their cherished theory can survive the kind of teaching that encourages critical thinking.[19]

I do not know whether or not my reasoning will persuade the educators of Kansas or other states. If they do decide to go ahead with a propaganda campaign, they will have to wage it with half-educated graduates who have never learned the strongest arguments for the case they are supposed to refute, who have been taught to take for granted that the peppered moth experiment illustrates how you get moths, trees, birds and scientific observers in the first place. Science will gain nothing even if the educators do manage to browbeat the public into submission with weapons like that. You can't defend science by ruling important issues off the table, by ridiculing dissenters, or by keeping people from hearing the evidence for and against the currently prevailing theories. The kind of science that deserves to be defended isn't afraid to meet criticism with its own methods: reasoned argument, precise definitions, repeatable experiments, and an open mind about all questions that can't be settled by unbiased scientific testing. You can defend particular theories or institutions by methods other than the genuine methods of science, but if you take that road you will find eventually that what you are defending isn't science.

4

SCIENCE & MODERNIST THEOLOGY

Does Theology Provide Any Knowledge?

Ordinary and Elite Scientists

In 1914 and again in 1933[1] Bryn Mawr College psychology professor James Leuba surveyed the attitudes of scientists toward the kind of religion Philip Wentworth had learned as a youth, before he went to Harvard and converted to naturalism. Leuba obtained a random sample of names from *American Men of Science*, the standard reference directory, and within that sample set aside a group of "greater scientists," so designated in the directory by stars next to their names. Because he wanted to measure the prevalence of traditional, supernaturalist religious beliefs rather than the liberal or modernist variety that tends to be more attractive to intellectuals, Leuba asked his subjects two specific questions: Do you believe in (1) "a God in intellectual and affective communication with man . . . to whom one may pray in expectation of receiving an answer" and (2) "personal immortality." Responses were anonymous, and the only options were "yes," "no" and "don't know."

Some respondents complained that the implicit definition of religion was narrow, but of course it was meant to be. Leuba was testing his version of the hypothesis that modern knowledge leads inevitably to increasing secularization. He thought that progress in science would lead to "a revision of public opinion regarding . . . the two cardinal beliefs of official Christianity," namely, a prayer-answering God and a life after death. In other words, Leuba believed that educated people generally, and elite scientists in particular, would go through the same secularization process that Philip Wentworth experienced at Harvard, and that this would cause them either to leave the Christian faith altogether or to reinterpret its main tenets to discard the supernatural elements. As Wentworth himself put it, secularized Christians would believe at most in "a God who had created the world and then left it to govern itself by natural law, . . . [so that] Prayers could not move him." Going that way, as Wentworth well knew, leads to agnosticism or atheism in the end even if it goes through a midpoint of liberal religion, which was once described by Charles Darwin's grandfather as "a bed to catch a falling Christian."

In 1914 about 40 percent of all the scientists answered yes to the two questions. Less than one-third of the "greater scientists" answered yes in 1914, and in 1933 more than 80 percent answered no to both questions. The difference between ordinary and greater scientists is not surprising, since the former category would include many who are basically teachers or who work with relatively narrow technological applications. The starred "greater scientists" were predominantly successful researchers in basic science, who could be expected to have a deeper understanding of the concepts behind science and their significance for religion.

In 1996 historian Edward Larson and journalist Larry Witham repeated Leuba's survey of scientists asking the same questions of a sample taken from the standard directory, now titled *American Men and Women of Science.* The first results were nearly identical to those in Leuba's 1914 survey: 40 percent of scientists-in-general still say they believe in a prayer-answering God and in personal immortality. This figure seemed to contradict Leuba's prediction of a secularizing trend, and some theistic evolutionists seized on it to argue that the scientific world is not overwhelmingly prejudiced in favor of naturalism. But in 1998 Larson and Witham repeated the survey for elite scientists, defined specifically (since the directory no longer gives stars to the greater scientists) as those who have been elected to membership in the National Academy of Sciences.[2] For this group the secularization hypothesis was abundantly confirmed. Disbelief in supernatural theism among Academy members was over 90 percent, and for biologists it was 95 percent. Remember, these responses were anonymous. If biologists had to stand up publicly in front of their scornful peers to answer, the percentage of avowed supernatural theists would probably be even smaller.

Larson and Witham reported their findings in a 1999 *Scientific American* article which included anecdotal information that summarized what just about everybody familiar with evolutionary science knows to be the case. Harvard professor Ernst Mayr, a National Academy member since 1954 and the acknowledged dean of evolutionary biologists (still active at the end of the century in his mid-nineties) had surveyed his own Harvard colleagues.

> "It turned out we were all atheists," he recalls. "I found that there were two sources." One Mayr typified as "Oh, I became an atheist very early. I just couldn't believe all that supernatural stuff." But others told him, "I just couldn't believe that there could be a God with all this evil in the world." Mayr adds, "Most atheists combine the two. The combination makes it impossible to believe in God."

That is what Mayr encountered at Harvard, but it is not the whole story. For example, one can find in Christian colleges many science teachers who passionately defend evolution because they want to save Christianity by reconciling it to a modern scientific worldview. Those colleges are very far down the academic pecking order from Harvard, however. Oxford University chemist Peter Atkins succinctly summarized the dominant view among elite scientists when a reporter asked him about the 40 percent figure in 1997: "You clearly can be a scientist and have religious beliefs. But I don't think you can be a scientist in the deepest sense of the word, because they are such alien categories of knowledge." Atkins was making the point that it is not any specific discovery that makes science so alien to supernatural religion but rather the naturalistic way of thinking that is second nature to evolutionary scientists. A person might believe in supernatural forces and still do experiments competently, but there would be ambivalence in her thinking that could limit her commitment to science. For comparison, consider the ambivalent position of an agnostic theologian. He might write competent scholarly papers on the fine points of the doctrine of justification by faith, but would he be a theologian in the deepest sense of the word if he had no experience of saving faith?

The Two-Platoon Strategy for Marginalizing Religion

Larson and Witham brought their findings right into the heart of the political effort by science organizations (especially the U.S. National Academy of Sciences) to portray "evolution" as having no important implications for religion. Their conclusion gains added weight because it appeared in *Scientific American,* one of the most secure bastions of scientific materialism:

"Whether God exists or not is a question about which science is neutral," the [National Academy's report on science education] cautiously begins, before launching its broadside of scientific arguments against religious objections to teaching evolution. But the irony is remarkable: a group of specialists who are nearly all unbelievers—and who believe that science compels such a conclusion—told the public that "science is neutral" on the God question. . . . "There are many outstanding members of this Academy who are very religious people, people who believe in evolution, many of them biologists," offered NAS president Bruce Alberts. Of course he did not claim that these "very religious" NAS members believed in a God as defined in Leuba's survey—traditional Jewish, Christian or Muslim theism, that is—but that would have been the natural interpretation of his statement by many in the general public.

Larson and Witham label as "irony" what seems more like deliberate deception to me. The National Academy's way of dealing with the religious implications of evolution is akin to the two-platoon system in American football. When the leading figures of evolutionary science feel free to say what they really believe, writers such as Edward O. Wilson, Richard Dawkins, Daniel Dennett, Carl Sagan, Steven Pinker, Stephen Jay Gould, Richard Lewontin and others state the "God is dead" thesis aggressively, invoking the authority of science to silence any theistic protest. That is the offensive platoon, and the National Academy never raises any objection to its promoting this worldview.

At other times, however, the scientific elite has to protect the teaching of the "fact of evolution" from objections by religious conservatives who know what the offensive platoon is saying and who argue that the science educators are insinuating a worldview that goes far beyond the data. When the objectors are too numerous or influential to be ignored, the defensive platoon takes the field. That is when we read those spin-doctored reassurances saying that many scientists are religious (in some sense), that science does not claim to have proved that God does not exist (but merely that he does not affect the natural world), and that science and religion are separate realms which should never be mixed (unless it is the materialists who are doing the mixing). Once the defensive platoon has done its job it leaves the field, and the offensive platoon goes right back to telling the public that science has shown that "God" is permanently out of business.

Theistic Modernists and Spinoza's God

Although the most prestigious evolutionary scientists are almost without exception agnostics or atheists, there are also a good many theologians and religiously inclined scientists who not only accept the theory of evolution but defend it vigorously. These are persons who have made the choice that Philip Wentworth rejected, to adopt and advocate a modernist worldview within the mainstream religious community. Among the better known of these theistic evolutionists are Ian Barbour, Nancey Murphy, Howard Van Till, Philip Hefner, Robert John Russell, Arthur Peacocke and John Haught. None of these is remotely as prominent as the leading members of evolutionary science's offensive platoon, but as a group—supported by the considerable financial resources of the John M. Templeton Foundation—they dominate the tiny segment of the academic world that is concerned with the relationship between science and religion. All accept methodological naturalism as the basis of scientific thinking, and therefore they also accept the neo-Darwinian picture of evolution as governed at all levels by some combination of physical law, chance and natural selection. They concede that evolution so defined has regularly been employed by scientists and philosophers to support atheism and to disparage theism, but they insist that this need not be so and argue that at a deeper level evolutionary science and nonfundamentalist theology are compatible and perhaps even mutually reinforcing.

As a rule, theistic modernists do not accept evolution grudgingly, nor do they dispute the Darwinian claim that evolution is undirected (at least as far as scientific evidence can determine). On the contrary, they embrace evolution with all its randomness as much for its theological merits as for its scientific standing. Some of them come close to saying that biological evolution is a fundamental doctrine of the Christian faith. I have observed that in some Christian academic circles it is considered far more offensive to deny the theory of evolution than it is to deny the divinity of Jesus or even the existence of God. The kind of academic thinking that lies behind that enthusiasm for evolution is well illustrated by Georgetown University theology professor John F. Haught, who writes that "evolution is an absolutely essential ingredient in our thinking about God today."[3] This is because

> if there exists a loving God who is intimately related to the world we should expect an aspect of indeterminacy or randomness in nature. The reason is simple: love typically operates not in a coercive but in a persuasive manner. . . . When viewed in a genuinely theistic perspective, then, there has to be room for uncertainty, i.e., an absence of direct divine determinism in the universe. . . . It is because God is a persuading love rather than a domineering force that the world not only evolves, but does so in an indeterminate manner.[4]

Some theological modernists are as strongly opposed to miracles as are scientific materialists because such an example of direct intervention would violate both the rational order established by the laws and the autonomy of nature that is permitted by chance. According to Arthur Peacocke, "A God who is a miracle-worker like that would not be worthy of worship."[5] If God did commit a miracle (like a physical resurrection, for example), Peacocke would apparently be offended enough to withdraw his allegiance. Other theistic evolutionists do accept individual miracles, although generally in a tentative or defensive way that suggests a certain embarrassment. Kenneth Miller, a Roman Catholic cell biologist and skilled platform debater for Darwinism, writes in his book *Finding Darwin's God* that

> a key doctrine in my own faith is that Jesus was born of a virgin, even though it makes no scientific sense—there is the matter of Jesus' Y-chromosome to account for. But that is the point. Miracles, by definition, do not have to make scientific sense. They are specific acts of God, designed in most cases to get a message across. Their very rarity is what makes them remarkable.[6]

I suspect that most of Miller's materialist colleagues will wonder how serious he can be in claiming to believe in an event while saying that it makes no scientific sense, especially since he is vigorous in judging all other claims of supernatural influence on the natural world by the standards of science. If he makes this one exception then why not others, and how does he decide where to draw the line? They may also wonder what Miller could possibly mean by his quest to "find Darwin's God," when it is so widely known in the scholarly world (and even to Miller himself) that Darwin in his later years was an agnostic.[7]

Probably the best way to explain why some theistic modernists are enthusiastic not only about evolution but specifically about *unguided* evolution is to start with Albert Einstein, who famously commented that "Science without religion is lame; religion without science is blind."[8] Einstein's frequently quoted references to God can give the unwary the impression that he believed in a supernatural creator, and this misunderstanding is exploited by Darwinists who want to reassure the religious public that scientists can be religious too. There is an enormous difference, however, between the

God of traditional biblical religion and a metaphorical "God" which is merely a reverent way of referring to the laws of nature or of giving a spiritual dimension to human reason. Einstein did not believe in a personal God but in what he called "Spinoza's God," an impersonal principle behind the laws akin to what Stephen Hawking must have meant when he said that a unified physical theory would permit us to "know the mind of God" or what Paul Davies means when he writes books with titles like *The Mind of God*. Spinoza denied the existence both of a cosmic purpose and of human free will because he thought that all things were subject to the laws of cause and effect. In 1932 Einstein wrote that "Spinoza was the first to apply with strict consistency the idea of an all-pervasive determinism to human thought, feeling and action. In my opinion, his point of view has not gained general acceptance by all those striving for clarity and logical rigor only because it requires not only consistency of thought but also unusual integrity, magnanimity and—modesty."[9] (Einstein was apparently unaware that his own statement was both immodest and self-contradictory, since praise or blame is meaningless if all human thought is governed by physical laws.) When Einstein opposed quantum indeterminacy because "God does not play dice," he meant only that he preferred to believe in a universe that is law-governed rather than chance-governed.

If inviolable laws govern all things, then there is no human freedom. For those who think in naturalistic categories, the only alternative to law is chance. That is why theological modernists have tended to see both Darwinian theory and quantum mechanics as liberating the cosmos from Spinoza's determinism. Kenneth Miller's biology text insists that "evolution works without plan or purpose."[10] To most people this sounds like agnosticism, but to theistic modernists it implies that the laws of nature do not foreordain everything after all but leave some of the most important things to the vagaries of chance. In that peculiar sense one can interpret Darwin as contributing to the project of theological modernism even though he was personally an agnostic. It is an illusion to imagine that this line of thought has anything to do with human free will or loving persuasion, however. A coin that may land heads or tails is no more free to choose between the two than is a weighted coin that always comes up heads. The power of rational choice does not exist where either chance or law determines every outcome.

Quantum mechanics also allows for a sort of miracle—defined as a statistical freak event rather like having a coin toss come up heads a million times in a row. The very atheistic Richard Dawkins wrote that the Statue of Liberty might wave her arm if all of the atoms just happened to move in the same direction once in a great while, although of course he wouldn't believe you for a moment if you said you saw the statue make the sign of the cross. So it is awkward but possible to be a modernist and yet preserve a space for individual miracles, provided that the miracles are always unfalsifiable and one does not insist that other people take them seriously. Of course most scientific materialists view miracle stories as pious legends and are typically either contemptuous or condescendingly tolerant toward people who claim to believe them, but they have no need to go to war over claims that are easily dismissed as self-deception.

Temporary and Permanent Gaps

Warfare does erupt whenever religious people claim that God has influenced the creation on a regular basis, in some manner that can be rationally supported and tested by scientific investigation. That is why the evidence for intelligent causes in biology is so much more threatening to the materialist worldview than a thousand miracle stories, and also why modernist theists so vehemently insist that such evidence cannot conceivably exist. The modernist doctrine is that theism must always yield to naturalism on any subject about which science has the power to investigate, because science will always provide a viable naturalistic explanation in the end. As Kenneth Miller puts it, "We are now far enough along in the development of science to appreciate that its track record suggests that ultimately it will find natural causes for natural phenomena." It follows that theists must avoid at all costs the "god of the gaps" fallacy, meaning that they should never attempt to take advantage of what can only be a *temporary* gap in the fabric of naturalistic explanation. For example, theistic modernists would never argue that God might have directly intervened in nature to produce the first living organism. Science may not be able to produce a credible theory of prebiological evolution just yet, but—*if Kenneth Miller is right about the track record*—such a theory is very likely to emerge in time. Whether the track record of naturalism in science is actually one of unbroken success would be highly debatable, if the rules of science allowed such a debate, but the rule that critics must accept methodological naturalism (on pain of being dismissed as creationists) makes it effectively impossible to audit the books.

Instead of pledging their credibility to those temporary gaps, which involve the risk of falsification, modernist theologians look for *permanent* gaps—those that are, in principle, outside the reach of scientific investigation. One such gap is at the ultimate beginning, when the laws of nature and the physical constants were set down. The ultimate beginning might be pushed back by theories involving multiple universes, but science will always have to start somewhere with something already in existence. God might find a permanent refuge from investigation in the time just before that somewhere. Another permanent gap might be at the level of quantum uncertainty. Quantum theory assumes that events at that level can be predicted only statistically, so there is in principle no way to predict the behavior of individual electrons or photons. Theistic modernists can therefore say that God made the laws in the first place and even that he affects reality nowadays by tweaking quantum events, without fear that scientific investigation will push the deity out of this last refuge. Perhaps on that basis modernist theologians can engage the scientific materialists in a constructive dialogue—*if* they reassure the materialists that they are not "fundamentalists" and that they accept methodological naturalism as the basis of scientific investigation. If theological modernists are willing to repudiate Genesis-as-history and intelligent-design-as-biology, will the scientific materialists allow them a place at the table?

Gould's NOMA: Separate but Equal

Not really, because the materialists see no need to make concessions to people whom they regard as either hopelessly wooly minded or yearning to find some opportunity to sneak some element of supernatural influence into science. The best terms theists are likely to get were offered by Stephen Jay Gould, president of the American Association for the Advancement of Science and successor to Ernst Mayr as Alexander Aggasiz Professor of Zoology at Harvard University. In one of his regular essays for *Natural History* magazine[11] Gould proposed a peace-making formula he called NOMA—nonoverlapping magisteria. *Magisterium* is Latin for "teaching authority"—specifically, the teaching authority of the Roman Catholic Church—a term which Gould chose because he framed his essay as a commentary on a statement by Pope John Paul II. Gould argued that the key to maintaining peace between science and religion is to recognize that each has its own distinct magisterium that the other must respect. The NOMA principle assigns to the realm of science questions relating to the empirical universe: "what is it made of (fact) and why does it work this way (theory)?" Questions regarding moral meaning and value go to religion. Gould explained that "to cite the arch clichés, we get the age of rocks, and religion retains the rock of ages; we study how the heavens go, and they determine how to go to heaven." Scientists violate this separation of magisteria when they claim a special authority over questions of morality or ultimate purposes; religious people trespass when they make factual claims that contradict the findings of science. Put so simply, Gould's NOMA may sound like a formula that respects the integrity of each sphere and sets the preconditions for a constructive and mutually respectful dialogue. But there is a catch.

Whenever one party to a conflict proposes to settle it with a formula of "separate but equal," the other party had better look carefully to see who is going to draw the boundary and where it is going to be drawn. In 1996 Pope John Paul II had partially defined the boundary in his message to the Pontifical Academy of Sciences, making two significant pronouncements concerning biological evolution. On the one hand, the pope said that the "theory of evolution" (which he did not define more precisely) is now "more than a hypothesis" because it has been confirmed by many independent lines of investigation. On the other hand, the pope went on to say that some versions of the theory of evolution are not strictly derived from data but also "borrow certain notions from natural philosophy. . . . Hence the existence of materialist, reductionist and spiritualist explanations." The pope set one specific limitation on all this scientific theorizing and philosophical speculation: "Theories of evolution which, in accordance with the philosophies inspiring them, consider the spirit as emerging from the forces of living matter or as a mere epiphenomenon of this matter, are incompatible with the truth about man."[12] To put the point more generally, the pope's version of NOMA drew a line between (1) legitimate scientific theories based on empirical evidence, which the Church will honor, and (2) overly ambitious manifestations of materialist philosophy which contradict truths which are fundamental to the Church's magisterium.

Gould responded to the pope as a conqueror might respond to a defeated enemy desperate to surrender on face-saving terms. To scientific materialists, empirical science and materialist explanation are virtually the same thing, and "outside of science" effectively means "outside of objective reality." Hence Gould predictably described the pope's first point as a decisive concession, and brushed aside the pope's second point as a sentimental attempt to dilute the force of the concession. Gould thought that the previous papal statement on evolution (Pius XII's *Humani Generis* in 1950) had only grudgingly allowed evolution as a legitimate but debatable hypothesis, whereas John Paul's statement had conceded the obvious—that "additional data and theory have placed the factuality of evolution beyond reasonable doubt." "Thanks for noticing," Gould commented condescendingly, and he went on to pronounce that "sincere Christians must now accept evolution not merely as a plausible possibility but also as an effectively proven fact." If they do not, then presumably they are not sincere Christians.

But what about the pope's second proposition, which challenged the extension of materialist philosophy to the soul? Gould briefly noted that the pope still maintained an "insistence on divine infusion of the soul." He described this quaint notion as having some possible "metaphorical value" but added that he *privately* suspects it to be "no more than a sop to our fears, a device for maintaining a belief in human superiority within an evolutionary world offering no privileged position to any creature." In short, the pope was committing the sin of anthropocentrism, or speciesism, considered by many Darwinists to be comparable to racism or homophobia. But in a significant amendment to his comment on this topic Gould added, "I also know that souls represent a subject outside the magisterium of science. My world cannot prove or disprove such a notion, and the concept of souls cannot threaten or impact my domain."

Those last words may have alarmed some of Gould's colleagues. Science has nothing to fear from a soul that is no more than a metaphor, but what if the magisterium of religion teaches that the soul and its supernatural creator are real entities whose existence is known by divine revelation rather than through the investigative methods of science? Once one divine revelation is allowed, others may follow. Such a source of knowledge would be far from harmless to the magisterium of science, which claims exclusive jurisdiction over all questions of fact. It is not merely a matter of letting a tiny bit of religion into a science-dominated world. *If heaven really exists,* then the authority to determine how to get to heaven is vastly more important than the authority to say how the mundane cosmos works, since the latter deals only with earthly knowledge that will soon pass away. On the other hand, *if heaven doesn't exist,* and if instead everything ends with the death of the material body, then the effort to get to heaven is a wild goose chase. To which magisterium does the authority to teach whether heaven is real or illusory belong? How is it determined whether divine revelation can be a foundation for knowledge? Anyone familiar with Gould's writing and the climate of opinion among elite scientists would have no doubt that Gould takes for granted that all such questions are within the magisterium of science and that all supernatural entities are therefore officially unreal. If there were any doubt about the matter, Gould removed it when he revised his essay for publication in book form. Using language appropriate for chiseling on stone tablets Gould declared what he frankly called a "limitation on concepts of God":

> The first commandment for all versions of NOMA might be summarized by stating: "Thou shalt not mix the magisteria by claiming that God directly ordains important events in the history of nature by special interference knowable only through revelation and not accessible to science."[13]

Gould wrote this scientific naturalist version of the First Commandment as if it came directly from the inherent nature of things, but of course it really is a power play emanating from the magisterium of science, as represented by Gould himself. Behind the power play stands a philosophy that bars religion from claiming that there is a supernatural creator (much less one who was incarnated in Jesus), a divinely infused soul, a life after physical death or a source of divine revelation such as inspired Scripture. This is "separate but equal" of the *apartheid* variety. If Gould's NOMA were a bus, there would be no doubt about who owns and drives the bus and who is required to ride only in the back seats. Gould's imperialism was a bit much even for John Haught, whose general principle is that religion should not only accept but enthusiastically *confirm* the claims of the scientific community about evolution. Haught wrote that "Gould never concedes the slightest cognitive status to religion or theology. . . . He never allows that religion can put us in touch with transcendental reality or, for that matter, give us anything resembling truth. . . . At best, religion paints a coat of 'value' over the otherwise valueless 'facts' disclosed by science. Religion can enshroud reality with 'meaning,' but, for Gould, this reality is purely of our own making."[14]

That is exactly right, and it is what not only Gould but the leaders of the National Academy of Sciences mean when they speak of religion and science as separate spheres. If Haught is unpleasantly surprised, it is because he was under the misapprehension that the Darwinists are engaged in objective fact-finding when they are really engaged in a campaign to establish a materialist definition of knowledge. They justify their monopoly position, when they are in a mood to be candid, on the ground that religion or theology is not entitled to any cognitive status because it provides no knowledge. It is science—founded on materialist premises—that discovered not only evolution but everything else that is known about the universe and about how human beings came into existence. All modernist theologians can do is to put a theistic spin on the story provided by materialism. They are not creating knowledge but merely borrowing knowledge to put a subjective interpretation on it.

Although Gould gave the realm of religion absolutely nothing in the end, he did try to sugarcoat the bitter pill, risking criticism from other prominent scientists who think it more honest (and perhaps more merciful in the long run) not to encourage the religious people in any false hopes that science will ever respect their empty realm. For example, Richard Dawkins commented that science is compatible with religion if the latter means only feelings of awe at the wonders of the universe or the fundamental laws of physics (that's basically what "Spinoza's God" means). But he added that such a flabby definition leaves no room whatsoever for a "hypothetical being who answers prayers, intervenes to save cancer patients or helps evolution over difficult jumps, forgives sins or dies for them." As for pretending to concede a separate magisterium to religion, Dawkins scornfully remarked that "such agnostic reconciliation is . . . easy to mistake for a genuine meeting of the minds."[15] In the end Dawkins differed from Gould only in that he expressed himself in more in-your-face language:

> Theologians should make a choice. You can claim your own magisterium, separate from science's but still deserving of respect. But in that case, you must renounce miracles. Or you can keep your

Lourdes and your miracles and enjoy their huge recruiting potential among the uneducated. But then you must kiss goodby to separate magisteria and your high-minded aspiration to converge with science.[16]

That ultimatum states a dilemma that is effectively no choice at all. If theologians claim that there *is* a supernatural reality, then they are at war with science. If they don't make that claim, then their "magisterium" has no independent source of knowledge and can only borrow from science. Either way, they have no cognitive status. The theologians may be perfectly willing to stick to saying how to go to heaven, and to leave it to the scientists to say how the heavens go. But the scientists insist that they concede that religion can't tell us how to go to heaven because no such place exists! This refusal to allow theology any cognitive territory is not something about which the magisterium of science (as defined by Gould, Dawkins and the National Academy) might be willing to negotiate because it is fundamental to their conception of what science *is*. The only difference of opinion is over whether to put the point bluntly or tactfully. If there is to be a dialogue between equal spheres rather than a domination of one sphere by the other, then religion must at a minimum propose an alternative to Gould's first commandment—perhaps in the following form:

Thou shalt not mix the magisteria by dressing naturalistic philosophy up as if it were science, and thou must learn to conduct impartial fact-finding independent of any philosophical dogmatism.

That would provide a starting point for a genuine dialogue about the difference between what evolutionary scientists want to believe and what the data actually indicate when interpreted without a materialist prejudice. Such a negative formulation—necessary as it is—is nonetheless insufficient to provide a basis for a separate magisterium of religion. Being a critic of philosophy dressed up as science is a worthy activity, but something more is needed if religion is to produce positive teaching. Of course religious people, as well as agnostics, can have their personal opinions about morality or the meaning of life. Even Dawkins and Gould are willing to concede that. But a teaching authority cannot be based on subjective feelings, ungrounded speculation or empty words. If theologians are to teach, they must have a source of knowledge independent of that possessed by science. And if they are going to assert the existence of such a cognitive territory, they must be prepared to defend it.

Teaching from a Foundation of Knowledge

Here is an example of the kind of teaching a Christian theologian* might offer as *knowledge,* meaning public truth to which everyone should pay heed. If this teaching is true, it is something that scientists (and everybody else) ought to know, and it is not something that anyone could learn from science. I do consider it to be true, but my point for now is merely to provide an example of the *kind* of teaching which theology has to be able to provide if it is to qualify as a realm of knowledge.

> And behold, a lawyer stood up to put [Jesus] to the test, saying "Teacher, what shall I do to inherit eternal life?" [Jesus] said to him, "What is written in the law? How do you read?" And he answered, "You shall love the Lord your God with all your heart, and with all your soul, and with all your strength, and with all your mind; and your neighbor as yourself." And [Jesus] said to him: "You have answered right; do this, and you will live." (Luke 10:25-28 RSV)

---

*Not all theologians are Christians, of course, but the debate over evolution is almost entirely carried on by materialists and Christians, or at least persons in the Christian tradition. Once we move from criticism of materialism to the beginning of a positive program, it is necessary to work from a specific basis rather than from the inherently vague platform of religion-in-general. In chapter seven I explain why the crucial question for me is not whether "religion" has some value but rather the question of Jesus: "Who do you say that I am?"

That is not a miracle story, nor does it encroach on the magisterium of science by setting any limits to empirical investigation. If we are to take the teaching seriously, however, we must make some important background assumptions that contradict the worldview presuppositions of the National Academy of Sciences. The teaching of the story makes sense as *knowledge* only if we assume that there really is such a thing as eternal life. We also must assume that there exists a text based ultimately on divine authority that instructs us—when interpreted by a competent teacher—how to obtain this eternal life. Third, we must assume that God is both real and involved with our lives to the extent that it is rational to love him with all our faculties. There is more, but you get the point. From a materialist viewpoint, eternal life is an illusion based on wishful thinking, and the "law" is a collection of long-outdated lore from a primitive society. It would be absurd to waste your life trying to love a being that is either nonexistent or at least impossibly distant and uninvolved with the world. The Westminster Shorter Catechism famously says, "Man's chief end is to glorify God and enjoy him forever." Materialist philosophy says on the contrary that humankind's chief intellectual end is to investigate, control and enjoy the material world, perceiving in the process that God is an entity existing only in the human imagination. If theologians are unwilling or unable to challenge the materialist definition of "knowledge" implicit in evolutionary science, then they deserve no more cognitive status than Gould and Dawkins are willing to give them.

Theologians need to defend their cognitive territory not only to establish a deity more substantial than Spinoza's (or Darwin's) God but because science itself requires the assistance of outside critics to check the tendency of ambitious scientists to go into the worldview business. A scientific community that is immune to outside criticism will be tempted to expand its territory and in the process will forsake rigorous scientific practice in order to justify conclusions that go far beyond what the data can justify. That is what has occurred in evolutionary science, and it is most spectacularly apparent when the materialists extend their territory to the human mind.

5

DARWINISM
OF THE MIND

Is the Thinking,
Choosing Self an Illusion?

The Selfish Gene and Robot Rebellion

Oxford University professor Richard Dawkins (whom we met previously in chapter two) is the world's most prominent exponent of Darwinism and scientific atheism. Evolution, according to Dawkins, is a story about competition among genes. Once upon a time chemicals somehow organized themselves into a DNA-based system that could reproduce itself. The first organism to emerge from the chemical soup was a naked gene, a length of genetic material that did little else but reproduce. But the naked gene spawned offspring, and thereafter mistakes in copying the genetic material created the variations on which natural selection could work its magic. In the fullness of time some of those offspring learned to build bodies (*phenotypes,* in scientific jargon). The only purpose of the bodies was to enable the genes to reproduce their own kind more effectively.* The genes that coded for the best bodies were thereby copied more effectively than their less successful rivals, and so bodies continually improved in form and function. Although there are powerful dissenters, gene selectionism is sufficiently dominant among evolutionary scientists that it is frequently referred to simply as "modern Darwinism."

From this basic theory that evolution is a process of gene selection it follows, to quote Dawkins's colorful prose, that humans (like other organisms) "are machines created by our genes. Like successful Chicago gangsters our genes have survived . . . in a highly competitive world. . . . I shall argue that a predominant quality to be expected in a successful gene is ruthless selfishness." Dawkins is here advancing a philosophical method called *reductionism*. Very complex sets of phenomena, such as human behavior in its entirely, are reduced to a single kind of material cause. When he is in his full reductionist flight Dawkins does not hesitate to draw the logical conclusion. "We are survival machines—robot vehicles programmed to preserve the selfish molecules known as genes."[1]

The logic implies that it may be only natural for robot vehicles to murder, rob, rape or enslave other robots to satisfy their genetic masters. Indeed, ruthless extermination of rival genes should be nearly as powerful an imperative as propagation of one's own. Modern Darwinism seems also to leave no basis for valuing the humane arts like poetry and music except to the extent that such things are useful in spreading the genes by (for example) building tribal solidarity. Nineteenth-century Darwinists, writing for European gentle-

---

*Dawkins and other gene selectionists frequently speak as if genes were thinking entities with purposes and plans, but this is merely a figure of speech. They mean that innovations such as phenotypes arise in the first instance by random mutation in a gene. If the innovation happens to result in more effective copying of the gene, then natural selection will preserve and spread the new feature. Any apparent reference to conscious purpose is purely metaphorical.

men who took their own social order for granted, might have been able to shrug aside such objections on the ground that science requires that we take an unsentimental view of the realities of life. Darwin himself coolly predicted in *The Descent of Man* that the most highly developed humans would soon exterminate the other races because that is how natural selection works.[2] Such casual references to genocide only began to seem reprehensible after Hitler, Stalin and Mao demonstrated what they meant in practice. Nowadays even the most uncompromising Darwinists have to make some concessions to morality, even at the cost of logical contradiction.

Modern Darwinists can respond that selfish genes do not always make selfish people, because it may be in the interests of the genes to encourage some forms of social cooperation, particularly within the family. According to the doctrine of "inclusive fitness," a mother might spread her own genes most effectively by sacrificing her own life to preserve the lives of her offspring, who carry the same genes. That's a pretty weak reassurance when contemplating the kinds of things that commissars and fuhrers tend to do, however, even if the mass murderers have an inclination to spare members of their immediate families. Stronger medicine is required if Darwinism is to avoid the obloquy that now attaches to "social Darwinism," and so Dawkins tries to square his gene theory with some acceptable morality by proposing a robot rebellion. He writes, "Let us try to *teach* generosity and altruism, because we are born selfish. Let us understand what our own selfish genes are up to, because we may then at least have the chance to upset their designs, something that no other species has ever aspired to."[3]

This is both scientifically absurd and morally naive. How could natural selection favor the development of a capacity to *thwart* the interests of the ruling genes? Any tendency to pursue goals other than gene copying would be self-extinguishing because by definition it would be less effective at spreading genetic copies. The genetic basis for this amazing capacity would have to emerge all at once, by what amounts to a materialist miracle, and then it would have to *evade* the destructive scrutiny of natural selection as it spread through the population. On the other hand, what *is* consistent with Darwinian logic is that gene selection might favor a talent for hypocrisy. If human nature is constructed by genes whose predominant quality is a ruthless selfishness, then pious lectures advocating qualities like generosity and altruism are probably just another strategy for spreading the selfish genes. Ruthless predators are often moralistic in appearance in order to disarm their intended victims. The genes that teach their robot vehicles not to take morality seriously but to take advantage of fools who *do* will have an advantage in the Darwinian copying competition. If you are preparing your son for a career with the mafia, you'd better not teach him to be loving and trusting. But you may teach him to feign loyalty while he is planning treachery. And if your daughter is planning a career writing popular books promoting gene selectionism, you may teach her to pretend to believe in morality even if she understands that her system implicitly excludes the concept.

Who or What Is the Self?

There is an even more fundamental problem with the robot rebellion, however. Just who is this "we" that is supposed to do the rebelling? Like other reductionists, Dawkins does not believe that there is a single, central self that utilizes the machinery of the brain for its own purposes. The central self that makes choices and then orders the body to act upon them is fundamentally a creationist notion, which reductionists ridicule as the "ghost in the machine," or the homunculus (little person) in the brain. Selfish genes would produce not a free-acting self but a set of mental reactions that compete with each other in the brain before a winner emerges to produce a bodily reaction that serves the overall interests of the genes. In the currently fashionable "computational" theory of the mind, as explicated by mind scientists such as Steven Pinker, the mind is a set of computers that solve specific problems forwarded by the senses. The "self" is at most a kind of coordinating function that prevents the parts from heading off in different directions.

At a joint lecture in 1999 Dawkins asked Pinker, "Am I right to think that the feeling I have that I'm a single entity, who makes decisions, and loves and hates and has political views and things is a kind of illusion that has come about because Darwinian selection found it expedient to create that illusion of unitariness rather than let us be a society of mind?" Pinker answered affirmatively that "the fact that the brain ultimately controls a body that has to be in one place at one time may impose the need for some kind of circuit . . . that coordinates the different agendas of the different parts of the brain to ensure that the whole body goes in one direction." That hypothetical circuit is all that remains of the illusion of a free-acting self.[4]

Susan Blackmore takes this logic even further in her book *The Meme Machine,* which comes with an introduction by Dawkins himself. Dawkins invented the concept of memes to extend Darwinism into the realm of ideas and expression. Memes are analogous to genes because they reproduce by being copied in brains and are altered by copying errors. As Blackmore describes it, "Everything you have learnt by copying it from someone else is a meme. This includes your habit of driving on the left or right, eating beans on toast, wearing jeans, or going on holiday. . . . Memes are 'inherited' when we copy someone else's action, when we pass on an idea or a story, when a book is printed, or when a radio program is broadcast. Memes vary because human imitation is far from perfect. . . .

Finally, there is memetic selection. Think of how many things you hear in a day, and how few you pass on to anyone else."

Dawkins originally proposed the meme idea cautiously, but his followers have made it the basis for a complete philosophy of mind. Just as the selfish genes (supposedly) make the body, selfish memes (supposedly also) make the mind. And just as genes explain (ultimately) everything about the body, memes explain (ultimately also) everything about the mind. Blackmore speculates that the brain evolved as a vehicle for spreading useful memes. As the selfish memes coevolve with each other, they form complex memetic systems like languages, religions, scientific theories and political ideologies. Their most powerful creation, however, is the illusion of the self. "We may feel as though we have a special little 'me' inside, who has sensations and consciousness, who lives my life, and makes my decisions. Yet, this does not fit with what we know about the brain." The self cannot rebel against the genes because *there is no self.* Blackmore puts the conclusion with crushing finality:

> Dawkins ends *The Selfish Gene* with his famous claim that "We, alone on earth, can rebel against the tyranny of the selfish replicators.' Yet, if we take his idea of memes seriously, and push it to its logical conclusion, we find that there is no one left to rebel.[5]

The potentially rebellious self is not the only casualty of memetic theory, however. By the same logic Darwinism itself is merely another one of those memes. Memes propagate not because they are true but because brains have some tendency to copy them, in the way they copy commercial jingles or jokes. Quality has no necessary connection with copying power. "Mary had a little lamb" is a more potent meme than Keats's "Ode on a Grecian Urn."

Dawkins likes to dismiss religion as a "computer virus of the mind," because he thinks it appeals to shallow thinkers who welcome a certain amount of self-deception. One could offer the same diagnosis of Darwinism. Certainly Dawkins himself has found it profitable to propound the theory to uncritical audiences. But one must be careful in broadcasting the Darwin meme because when pushed too far it leads to conclusions that even the most ardent Darwinists hesitate to defend in public, and to logical contradictions that undermine Darwinism itself. By failing to perceive these dangers Steven Pinker got himself into a mess when he tried to convince the public that there is a genetic basis for infanticide.

Evolutionary Psychology Explains Infanticide

Newspapers in 1996-1997 reported two particularly shocking cases of infanticide. In one, a pair of eighteen-year-old college sweethearts delivered their baby in a hotel room, killed him and left the body in a dumpster. In the other, an eighteen-year old briefly left her high school prom to deliver her baby in a bathroom stall, left the infant dead in a garbage can and returned to the dance floor. Both events led to convictions for homicide. Conventional explanations attributed the crimes either to moral failure (personal or social) or to some form of mental pathology.

Steven Pinker, professor of psychology at the Massachusetts Institute of Psychology and a leading popularizer of evolutionary psychology, had a different kind of explanation: a genetic imperative. Writing in the *New York Times* Pinker argued that what he termed neonaticide (the killing of a baby on the day of its birth) is not attributable to mental illness because "it has been practiced and accepted in most cultures throughout history." Rather, a capacity for neonaticide is hard-wired into the maternal genes by our evolutionary history. Mothers in primitive conditions had to make hard choices between caring adequately for their existing infants and nurturing a newborn, and so "if a newborn is sickly, or if its survival is not promising, they may cut their losses and favor the healthiest in the litter or try again later on." According to Pinker the same genetic disposition may trigger neonaticide in any case where the pregnancy is threatening to the mother, such as where she has to conceal the pregnancy and possibly give birth alone or in dangerous circumstances. For this reason Pinker hypothesized that various cultural practices and psychological conditions protect the mother from too great an immediate attachment to an infant who may have to be sacrificed. "A new mother will first coolly assess the infant and her current situation and only in the next few days begin to see it as a unique and wonderful individual." In those first few days, it would seem killing an unwelcome infant would be perfectly natural and appropriate. And yet Pinker also wrote that "killing a baby is an immoral act," and that "to understand is not necessarily to forgive." Readers wondered what he could possibly have meant by these words. Do we perhaps have a "gene for justice" that causes us to impose retributive punishment on a mother whose gene for neonaticide causes her to kill her baby?

Pinker's reasoning attracted some harsh criticism. Michael Kelly in the *Washington Post* wrote that Pinker "did not go quite so far as to openly recommend the murder of infants. . . . But close enough, close enough."[6] Pinker responded indignantly by repeating the qualifications he had inserted in the original piece: killing is immoral, and to understand is not to forgive.[7] But in what sense can any conduct be immoral if it is a product of a genetic imperative? Pinker's astonishing answer (in his book) was that moral reasoning requires that we assume the existence of things which science tells us are unreal. "Ethical theory," he wrote, "requires idealizations like free, sentient, rational, equivalent agents whose behavior is uncaused, and its conclusions can be sound and useful even though the world, as seen by science, does not really have uncaused events. . . . A human

being is simultaneously a machine and a sentient free agent, depend-
ing on the purpose of the discussion."[8]

That may seem self-contradictory, but perhaps it is worse than
that. What Pinker may mean is that morality is founded on a "noble
lie" that the intellectual priesthood tells to the common people. Of
course the priests themselves know the lie for what it is and do not
recognize it as a limit on their own thinking or conduct, but they
conceal their nihilism by pretending to believe in conventional
morality. This is the same pretense Philip Wentworth had in mind
when he wrote that the myth of supernatural religion with its stern
father-figure in the sky may still be necessary to discipline the multi-
tudes who are incapable of self-control. For the same reason Voltaire
reportedly took care that his servants didn't hear the conversation at
the dinner table for fear they would steal the spoons. Much the same
theme is at the center of Dostoevsky's novels *Crime and Punishment*
and *The Brothers Karamazov*, in which the student Raskolnikov and
the servant Smerdyakov each committed murder because they acted
on the nihilistic philosophies they learned from intellectuals. Now
that these philosophies are promoted in the mass media, we may
expect many more people to apply the logic of nihilism to their own
conduct.

Andrew Ferguson of *The Weekly Standard*[9] followed up Kelly's
accusation with a devastating review of Pinker's logic, noting particularly the very weak anthropological evidence that Pinker cited in
support of his expansive conclusions. Basically, evolutionary psychology proceeds by erecting a mountain of speculation on the basis
of fragmentary evidence about primitive cultures. In Ferguson's
words, "Conjecture solidifies into fact; the fact then becomes a basis
for further conjecture, which evolves into another factual premise,
and so on." Besides the shaky factual premises, there is the inherent
absurdity of a discipline that can explain any behavior pattern *and*

its direct opposite equally well. If mothers protect and nurture their infants, that behavior exemplifies the maternal instinct that is produced by natural selection. If they kill their infants, then *that* behavior illustrates the neonaticidal instinct—which is also produced by natural selection. Like psychoanalysis, evolutionary biology can explain equally well why a man will betray his closest friends or why he will sacrifice his life to save a stranger. Experience with other pseudosciences, particularly Freudianism and Marxism, has taught the critical audience that a theory that explains everything explains nothing.

Is It Wrong to Kill Babies?

These methodological deficiencies of evolutionary psychology are notorious, although similar pseudoscientific practices go unnoticed when Darwinists stick to explaining the body. Pinker did not defend his factual assumptions or methodology when he responded to Ferguson's review, but he did defend himself on the moral question. Ferguson had pointed out that Pinker's logic closely tracked that of philosopher Michael Tooley, who has unapologetically argued that it is not intrinsically wrong to kill human infants before they attain "at least a limited capacity for thought" and thus become "quasi-persons," at about the age of three months. Before that time their capacities do not significantly exceed those of animals, and so they have no right to life greater than that of animals. Pinker endorsed the logic but merely refrained from drawing the inevitable conclusion that infanticide is morally unobjectionable, probably because he thought his readers were not ready for the bottom line—*yet.*

This point deserves emphasis because it illustrates how Darwinian logic works and why it fools so many people who are all too willing to be fooled. We saw in the previous chapter that the representatives of the scientific elite overwhelmingly reject any form of supernatural religion *and believe that science compels that rejection*. Nonetheless, they consider that they are not saying anything "about God" if at that precise moment they do not explicitly draw the conclusion that God is dead, or if they leave room for some form of modernist theology. Hence they indignantly reject any accusation that by teaching "evolution" they are undermining the belief that we are created by God. Their indignation is echoed by many theistic evolutionists, who take any criticism of Darwinian logic as an attack on their own sincerity.

The important thing is not the conclusion that scientific materialists are drawing today, however, but the conclusion that they will draw tomorrow on the basis of the logic that they are insinuating today. For a time they may say that science and religion are separate realms, with science owning the realm of fact and religion belonging to the realm of subjective opinion. Once this division is accepted, they will point out that it implies that religion has no access to knowledge, and so its realm is effectively empty. Today evolutionary psychologists may say that killing infants is wrong, but (in Andrew Ferguson's words) "they make us see it not as a moral horror, but as a genetically encoded evolutionary adaptation, as unavoidable as depth perception or opposable thumbs." Tomorrow they will say that the points you conceded yesterday establish that infanticide is not wrong after all. Whenever the "separate realms" logic surfaces, you can be sure that the wording implies that there is a ruling realm (founded on reality) and a subordinate realm (founded on illusions which must be retained for the time being). The formula allows the ruling realm to expand its territory at will.

For example, Pinker explained the basis of morality by reasoning that "science and morality are separate spheres of reasoning. Only by recognizing them as separate can we have them both."[10] Readers will recognize that this is exactly the formula by which Stephen Jay

Gould related science and religion, and it has the same consequences. When the time is right to overthrow some traditional moral
restriction, evolutionary psychologists will complete the logic by
observing that the moral sphere is as empty as the religious realm.
After all, both religion and morality rest on assumptions that science
has shown to be false. How can any authority be real if it is founded
on unreality?

We can see exactly this process operating in Pinker's reply to
Andrew Ferguson. First, Pinker demolished the idea that there is any
clear line between those who have a right to life and those who
don't:

> If you believe the right to life inheres in being sentient, you must
> conclude that a hamburger-eater is a party to murder. If you believe it
> inheres in being a member of Homo sapiens, you are just a species
> bigot. If you think it begins with conception, you should prosecute
> IUD users for murder and divert medical research from preventing
> cancer and heart disease to preventing the spontaneous miscarriages
> of vast numbers of microscopic conceptuses. If you think it begins at
> birth, you should allow abortion minutes before birth, despite the
> lack of any significant difference between a late-term fetus and a neo-
> nate.[11]

Pinker repeated his *pro forma* disclaimer that neonaticide is an
immoral act which should not be decriminalized, but his logic
implied that what is really immoral is the "species bigotry" that
holds that there is a moral difference between killing a baby and
killing an unwanted kitten. If the line between persons and nonper-
sons is inherently arbitrary, then the boundary can be moved at any
time if it becomes convenient to expand the category of members of
Homo sapiens who do not have a right to life. After all, Pinker himself believes that our sense of personhood is merely a circuit that the
genes create to ensure that the whole body goes in one direction. As

for relying on religion for guidance, Pinker scornfully commented, "That solution has given us stonings, witch-burnings, crusades, inquisitions, jihads, fatwas, suicide bombers, abortion-clinic gunmen, and mothers who drown their sons so they can be happily reunited in heaven." So that religion has no more standing in discussions of morality than it does in science. Pinker nailed the point down:

> Secular thinkers are prepared to struggle with difficult moral questions by reasoning them out on moral grounds, while welcoming our increasing knowledge about the brain. Ferguson instead seems to want to root morality on the theory that a deity injects a fertilized ovum with a ghostly substance, which registers the world, pulls the levers of behavior, and leaks out at the moment of death. Unfortunately for that theory, brain science has shown that the mind is what the brain does. The supposedly immaterial soul can be bisected with a knife, altered by chemicals, turned on or off by electricity, and extinguished by a sharp blow or a lack of oxygen. Centuries ago it was unwise to ground morality on the dogma that the earth sat at the center of the universe. It is just as unwise today to ground it on dogmas about souls endowed by God.

In that case it is equally unwise to ground morality on the dogma that there is a self that reasons and makes moral choices. After all, state-of-the-art neuroscience has proved that you can extinguish this so-called self by a sharp blow or a lack of oxygen, which proves that it is merely highly organized matter. If you follow the materialist logic through to the end, as Pinker and Susan Blackmore have done, you will conclude that the personal self in which we put so much stock is no more than an illusion. And if the right to life is founded on personhood rather than on mere membership in the species Homo sapiens, then nobody has a right to life. The logic that justifies neonaticide likewise justifies the slaughter of healthy adults.

The Mind-Brain Dilemma

Steven Pinker's understanding of mind and morality is a swamp of confusion, but he is also a central figure in evolutionary mind-science with a large and enthusiastic following. If his conclusions seem outrageous, it is merely because he is more candid than many others in drawing out the logical implications which are inherent in Darwinism of the mind. The dilemma that makes Pinker's thought so confused is also present in the work of some far more sophisticated academic theorists of neuroscience and its philosophy. They struggle with what is termed the "hard problem" of mind-science: how it is possible for material events in the brain to produce subjective conscious experience in the mind. If the brain is fundamentally a computer or group of computers, then a sensory input can produce an output (for example, lack of water can stimulate cells to invoke a mechanism to cause drinking). But computers do this without having any conscious awareness. Why aren't people like computers in this respect?

The confusion that the hard problem stimulates is illustrated by the contrasting views of two leading philosophers of mind, John Searle[12] and Paul Churchland, who could be described as the bookends marking the boundaries of the materialist viewpoint on the subject. Churchland champions "eliminative materialism," which holds that mental states do not exist.[13] When we speak of people having beliefs, thoughts, desires and sensations, or making decisions based on reflection, we are engaging in a kind of fiction termed "folk psychology." According to eliminative materialists, such mental entities are as unreal as ghosts or fairies. The goal of neuroscience is to replace the primitive folk-psychological talk with scientific descriptions of the nervous system's physical mechanisms such as patterns of activation in populations of neurons. Don't bother to object that eliminative materialism conflicts with common sense. Of course it does, but to eliminative materialists common sense is just one of those fictitious categories that a mature neuroscience will eliminate.

This bizarre theory is merely the *reductio ad absurdum* of materialism. If in the beginning were the particles, chance and the laws of physics—*and nothing else*—then everything that has happened since must be the products of those fundamental causal factors. No God or nonmaterial vital essence or "ghost in the machine" can possibly intrude. In that case it is logically inevitable that our mental activity can *in principle* be explained solely on the basis of physical causes, regardless of how far from a solution we may be at the present time. "If you don't like our conclusions," an eliminative materialist can argue, "then try to find an alternative set of assumptions that is acceptable to science." The irony is that eliminative materialism itself is fatal to science, since it implies that even the scientists are not really conscious and that their boasted rationality is really rationalization. In that case, why imagine that scientific reasoning can make true statements about ultimate reality? Extreme forms of modernist rationalism thus merge seamlessly with postmodernist relativism.

John Searle is as dedicated to materialism and Darwinism as Paul Churchland. He insists that among respectable thinkers, two theories are "not up for grabs." ("Not up for grabs" is Searle's way of announcing a foundational dogma that may not be disputed.) They are the atomic theory of matter (the world is made of particles) and the evolutionary theory of biology (life was made by a combination of matter, law and chance). Like all materialists Searle rejects dualism, the belief that there is some nonmaterial substance involved with the life processes, and he dismisses all talk of God in terms as hostile, and as simplistic, as those of Richard Dawkins himself. He describes two preposterous medieval miracle stories as if they exemplified religious belief, and then remarks that "educated members of society" no longer see supernatural meaning in things they don't understand. It follows for Searle as much as for Churchland that the mind also has to be the product of material causes—*and nothing else.* "We know for a fact that all of our conscious states are caused by brain processes. This proposition is not up for grabs."[14] We know this for a fact even though nobody knows how brain processes can cause conscious states because intellectual gatekeepers (including Searle himself) have decided to exclude from the academic conversation anybody who dares to question materialism.

On the other hand, Searle is equally dedicated to the principles of enlightenment rationalism, including the view that our minds have access to a reality "out there," and he insists that our subjective experience of consciousness is just as real an entity as the material processes from which it springs. These commitments are contradictory if our thoughts are in principle fully describable as the firing of various sets of neurons. So to save the higher level of mental activity Searle insists that first person conscious states of mind (I think and feel) are inherently incapable of being reduced to the material, third-person brain processes that neuroscience studies. They are "emergent" properties that arise not from the primary components of the brain in isolation, but in some mysterious way from combining those components into a complex organ. Searle admits that many of his critics have difficulty seeing how this doctrine of "non-reductive materialism" differs from outright dualism, since the chasm between the material process and the subjective experience seems to be forever unbridgeable. We may recall Pope John Paul II's caveat that "theories of evolution which, in accordance with the philosophies inspiring them, consider the spirit as emerging from the forces of living matter or as a mere epiphenomenon of this matter, are incompatible with the truth about man." John Searle splits the difference, saying that the mind *emerges* from the forces of living matter but is nonetheless not a mere epiphenomenon of this matter. You can imagine what consistent materialists think of that reasoning. They think that an unexplained and unexplainable leap from matter to mind is an evasion of the mind-brain problem, not a solution to it.

Information and the Mind

Science writer John Horgan's book *The Undiscovered Mind* carries a subtitle which explains its message: "How the human brain defies replication, medication, and explanation."[15] Mind-science is in a preparadigmatic state, in which various competing approaches each have their enthusiastic proponents and no one way of thinking about the subject is able to achieve predominance. We have already seen some of the major drawbacks of evolutionary psychology and materialist neuroscience. As these drawbacks are recognized, older theories look a bit better in contrast. Freudian psychiatry, on the ropes when its overblown scientific pretensions were shown in the 1980s to be illusory, is still in the field and making a slight comeback. Even once-discredited practices like lobotomies and electroshock therapy remain in use for extreme cases, nothing better having been discovered. Media-hyped wonder drugs like Prozac have been shown in controlled trials to be no more effective than a placebo. Above all, there is the baffling phenomenon of consciousness, which can still be summed up by Thomas Huxley's nineteenth century remark: "How it is that anything so remarkable as a state of consciousness comes about as a result of irritating nervous tissue, is just as unaccountable as the appearance of the Djin, when Aladdin rubbed his lamp."[16]

The absence of a breakthrough does not mean that the scientists are inactive or incompetent. On the contrary, late twentieth century technology has enabled them to make astounding discoveries. The problem is that the discoveries tend to deepen the underlying mystery by revealing ever more astounding levels of complexity. Horgan wonders whether mind-science will always be an enterprise in which different kinds of interesting stories can be told, all of them insightful up to a point but none of them adequate to explain more than a small part of the territory. Horgan notes the reductionist vision of Francis Crick, who tells his readers that "your joys and your sorrows, your memories and your ambitions, your sense of personal identity and free will, are in fact no more than the behavior of a vast assembly of nerve cells and their associated molecules." My own response to such talk would be to ask Crick if he thinks his own thoughts are reducible to a bunch of firing neurons, and if so, why he imagines that his thoughts are rational. Horgan is more accepting of reductionist talk, but still recognizes it as unilluminating:

> In a sense, Crick is right. We are nothing but a pack of neurons. At the same time, neuroscience has so far proved to be oddly unsatisfactory. Explaining the mind in terms of neurons has not yielded much more insight or benefit than explaining the mind in terms of quarks and electrons. There are many alternative reductionisms. We are nothing but a pack of idiosyncratic genes. We are nothing but a pack of adaptations sculpted by natural selection. We are nothing but a pack of computational devices dedicated to different tasks. We are nothing but a pack of sexual neuroses. These proclamations, like Crick's, are all defensible, and they are all inadequate.[17]

Of course they are inadequate. There are at least two reasons for the inadequacy, one scientific and the other philosophical. Let's start with the former.

Science Needs to Recognize Information for What It Is
Both Churchland and Searle assume that the choice before them is between material factors that can be investigated and ghostly, super-

natural factors that bring scientific advance to a standstill. This is a false duality. The real duality at every level of biology is the duality of matter and information. The philosophers of mind-science fail to understand the true character of information because they assume that it is produced by a material (i.e., Darwinian) process and hence is not something fundamentally different from matter. But this is merely a prejudice that would be swept away by unbiased thinking. *There is no scientific evidence that the brain, or any individual cell within the brain, either was or could have been created by matter unassisted by preexisting intelligence. The scientists who believe that natural selection made the brain do so not because of the evidence but in spite of the evidence.*

Once the materialist prejudice is put aside, a new way of understanding the subject emerges. What makes the mind from the brain is not the neurons but the information that coordinates the neurons and uses them (and perhaps other entities as yet unknown) to produce the phenomena of our mental life. To say that is not to offer a solution but rather to offer a way to take the first steps out of an impasse. Information is not matter, although it is imprinted in matter. It comes from elsewhere, from an intelligence that is so far (and perhaps forever) outside the ken of a science that examines only material entities and effects. The task of neuroscience is not to deny the reality of information or to insist in the teeth of the evidence that all information is the creation of some combination of physical law and chance, but to learn as much as possible about how the information interacts with matter to produce mental phenomena. Putting aside the overweening ambitions of mind-science is the first step toward a realistic science that recognizes its inherent limitations, and this brings us to the second step.

Science Must Recognize Its Inherent Limitations

When the metaphysicians of science concede that science has its limitations, they usually mean that *reality* and not science is what is limited. Because science has to be able to explain everything, reality has to be limited to those things that science can explain. Because science understands only material causes, whatever cannot be reduced to material causes has to be ignored, whether it be complex specified aperiodic genetic information, or irreducibly complex organs, or consciousness itself. Those like John Searle who wish to save the mind from this reductionism have to erect arbitrary barriers because to challenge materialism itself would be to incur expulsion from the academic conversation. Even theologians give in to the pressure, effectively conceding that materialism is true and then trying to preserve some remnant of the divine presence by making it unfalsifiable and hence uninteresting. Books like Edward O. Wilson's *Consilience* assert unabashedly that religion, literature, art, philosophy and law must conform to the materialist philosophy that rules the scientific community and must accept that Darwinism is the starting point for every human activity. Such imperialism is preposterous coming from a territory that is itself mired in confusion and contradiction, and yet *Consilience* was not only taken seriously but promoted with enthusiasm by adoring journalists.[18]

It is time for an effective challenge to this constricting, authoritarian, self-contradictory ideology. Providing that challenge is what the Wedge is all about.

6

THE EMPIRE
STRIKES BACK

*What Are the Arguments
Against Intelligent Design?*

The Critics

The intelligent design movement is usually ignored in the mainstream news media because journalists have been trained to portray the dispute over evolution as one between impartial scientific investigators on the one hand and poorly educated biblical fundamentalists on the other. Professors who dispute Darwinism because the scientific evidence is against it are not yet on their mental map. Nonetheless, Michael Behe, William Dembski and I have gained sufficient recognition and public support through our books and lectures that book-length refutations are beginning to appear. Two books in particular were published in 1999: College of New Jersey philosophy professor Robert Pennock's *Tower of Babel: The Evidence Against the New Creationism* and Brown University biology professor Kenneth R. Miller's *Finding Darwin's God: A Scientist's Search for Common Ground Between God and Evolution.* Miller is one of Darwinism's most effective debaters, and Pennock's book has impressive endorsements, including a recommendation from the National Academy of Sciences. These books represent the best that Darwinists have been able to do in meeting the arguments for intelligent design.

Both books simply refuse to take seriously any arguments against Darwinism or materialism, relying heavily on caricatures, ridicule and the strong negative implications of the term *creationism*. The basic line of attack is that any dissent from evolutionary naturalism is founded not on scientific evidence but on religious prejudice. Pennock and Miller also make specific arguments that deserve to be taken seriously, however. I'll respond to these after first briefly restating the case for intelligent design in biology, so readers will have clearly in mind just what Pennock and Miller are supposed to be refuting.

The Case for Intelligent Design[*]

A good place to begin is with the acknowledgment by Richard Dawkins that "Biology is the study of complicated things that give the appearance of having been designed for a purpose." More precisely, all living organisms are characterized by immense amounts of genetic information that enable them to function. Dawkins puts it vividly:

> Physics books may be complicated, but . . . the objects and phenomena that a physics book describes are simpler than a single cell in the body of its author. And the author consists of trillions of those cells, many of them different from each other, organized with intricate architecture and precision-engineering into a working machine capable of writing a book. . . . Each nucleus . . . contains a digitally coded database larger, in information content, that all 30 volumes of the *Encyclopedia Britannica* put together. And this figure is for *each* cell, not all the cells of the body put together.[1]

---

*For a much more complete explanation, see William Dembski, *Intelligent Design: The Bridge Betwen Science & Theology* (Downers Grove, Ill.: InterVarsity Press, 1999).

In short, the very complex processes of the cell must be directed by some information-rich entity that can be likened to a computer program. As I explained in chapter two, the information that directs the life processes—like any other meaningful text—needs to be *complex, aperiodic* and *specified.* The first requirement means that a very long string of letters or symbols is required. The second means that the order of the letters is not directed by physical or chemical laws, which by their nature produce only simply repeating patterns (such as printing "ABC" over and over again until the printer runs out of paper). The third requirement means that not just any order will do but only the precise order required to produce the encyclopedia, or the computer operating program, or the array of cellular proteins coded for in the DNA nucleotides. Genuinely creative evolution thus requires a mechanism capable of creating immense amounts of complex specified aperiodic genetic information. Random mutation is not such a mechanism, nor is natural selection, nor is any physical or chemical law. Laws produce simple repetitive order, and chance produces meaningless disorder. When combined, law and chance work against each other to prevent the emergence of a meaningful sequence.* In all human experience, only intelligent agency can write an encyclopedia or computer program, or produce complex specified aperiodic information in any form. Therefore, the information necessarily present in organisms points to the conclusion that they are products of intelligent design.

The concept of intelligent design does not rule out "evolution" in

---

*That is why the classic "monkeys at a typewriter" illustration oversimplifies the problem. Even if a random choice of letters could produce a specified text in a finite period of time, the fixed arrangement of letters on the keyboard would cause some letters (for example "G" "H" "J" and "K") to appear together very frequently, producing recurrent nonsense sequences like "hjk." In addition, crucial information (i.e., the English alphabet) is built into the situation by the keyboard. Give the monkey paper and pencil and he produces only meaningless squiggles instead of letters. Invention of the alphabet required human intelligence.

the sense of variation or diversification. Many examples of variation within the type occur, and humans by selective breeding produce impressive varieties of dogs and roses. (Selective breeding is itself a form of intelligent design, however, because the breeders employ purposeful intelligence and protect the overspecialized breeds from the natural selection that would otherwise eliminate them.) These uncontroversial examples of what is commonly termed "microevolution" involve no increases in genetic information and hence are not creative in the important sense. Reference to intelligent causes is indispensable not to account for mere *change* but to account for the creation of new complex genetic information. One convenient way of expressing this distinction is to say that the standard examples of microevolution are all of *horizontal* evolution, while the grand creative process should be called *vertical* evolution.

Whatever the terminology, the essential point is that something besides mere "change" is required to create new complex organs, and that something must be capable of a task equivalent to writing a computer operating program or an encyclopedia. Unless biologists can provide a testable mechanism capable of doing the job, then the correct scientific conclusion is that biological creation is an unsolved mystery. Calling the mystery "evolution" provides only the illusion of an explanation unless there is a specific theory available to explain how the required transformations are possible.[2] Neo-Darwinism is specific enough, but it doesn't fit the facts, and its mechanism has no real creative power.

A wise proverb warns that "it isn't what you don't know that gets you in trouble, it is what you *do* know that isn't so." Often the first step toward true understanding is to eliminate false concepts that merely conceal our ignorance by, for example, encouraging the belief that cyclical variations in finch beaks illustrates how birds came into existence in the first place. Science should never fear honest intellectual tools such as precise use of terms, unbiased investigation of evidence and refusal to accept unjustified extrapolations. If use of those tools leads to the undermining of a cherished theory, then that is a gain and not a loss for the advance of knowledge—even if it leaves scientists bewildered for a time. If no true answer is available, it is not an advance in knowledge to embrace a false answer.

Finally, intelligent design theorists need to explain why the vast majority of evolutionary scientists refuse to consider evidence of intelligent design in biology, scornfully dismissing the entire concept as "religion" rather than "science." This is because they identify science with naturalism, meaning that only "natural" (i.e., material or physical) forces may play a role in the history of life.[3] Where the designer is itself some natural entity, such as a human being, evidence for design is welcome. Space aliens are also permissible entities, and so Carl Sagan's Search for Extra-Terrestrial Intelligence (SETI) radio telescopes scan the sky for signals, which they could identify as products of intelligence by precisely the same methods which intelligent design theory applies to biology. The difference is that scientific naturalists *want* to find evidence for extraterrestrial life, in part because they would count it as evidence that natural laws produce life wherever favorable conditions exist and hence as clinching the case for naturalism. They don't want to find evidence for what they think of as an "interfering" God, meaning a God who does not leave everything to law and chance. Hence they will refuse to see evidence of design that is staring them in the face until they are reassured that the designer is something whose existence they are willing to recognize.

That is the case *for* intelligent design in biology. Now we turn to the critics.

A Darwinist Responds: Kenneth Miller

Kenneth Miller begins by defending the identification of science with materialism. He argues that any alternative to materialism in science could only involve an arbitrary refusal to consider evidence and a determination to substitute "miracle" for factual investigation:

> If I wanted to oppose the assumption of materialism, I might walk into a meeting of solar physicists, for example, and claim that the sun does not contain helium. Someone in the group would be likely to ask a simple question: "How, then, do you explain the 587.6 nanometer emission peak in the solar atmosphere?" My response: I do not have to explain it! Light from the sun, I would claim, is a miracle. Supernatural forces are responsible for that light, and such forces are beyond scientific explanation. "You'd might as well admit," I would insist, "that my explanation is just as good as yours. The only difference is that you pretend to be objective when you are not. Your so-called scientific work has a hidden, underlying bias in favor of scientific materialism. I have no such bias. Indeed, I'm the one with a truly open mind, because I can admit the possibility of the miraculous when you cannot."[4]

If I were willing to stoop to that level of caricature, I suppose I could portray Miller as insisting that the scientific instruments that measured the emission peak were designed by unintelligent natural forces and contemptuously rejecting as "religion" any attempt to assert the existence of engineers. The intelligent design position is not that miracles should be arbitrarily invoked in place of logical inferences from evidence, but rather that evidence pointing to intelligent causes, where present, should not be disregarded due to bias. Miller either does not know, or chooses to ignore, that the argument for intelligent design rests primarily on the existence of complex genetic information and the absence of a natural mechanism for creating it. The 587.6 nanometer emission peak is an example of a law-like regularity produced by a known physical process. Recognizing such a regularity is fully consistent with the case for intelligent

design in biology and involves no necessary adherence to materialism.

Consistent with that initial basic misunderstanding, Miller gro-
tesquely distorts the design concept by insisting that it must apply
either to everything or to nothing, when in fact the starting point for
intelligent design theory is that we can distinguish between entities
which are designed and those that are not. In Miller's words, "if
Johnson is right, then we should apply the explanation of design to
every event in the natural history of the planet. It is not logically tenable to allow that evolution could have produced some species but
not others; therefore, the explanation of design must be invoked for
the origin of every species."[5] This "all or nothing" standard is utter
nonsense. In the first place, it is only Darwinists who think that what
evolutionary theory needs to explain is primarily *speciation,* meaning the origin of a new species. A species (as most commonly
defined) is merely a reproductively isolated population, and such
isolation or loss of reproductive capacity does not necessarily
require any increase in genetic information. For example, two fruit
fly populations that cannot interbreed may be classified as separate
species although they are otherwise physically similar. Intelligent
design theorists are not concerned with whether natural variation
can produce reproductive isolation. We are concerned with the much
more important question of the origin of irreducibly complex systems or new complex genetic information. Far from saying that
everything is designed, design theory says that chance, law and
design all operate in the world and that it is possible to distinguish
between innovative changes that require design and variations which
can be produced by some combination of law and chance.

Because Miller does not recognize the problem of information
creation, he thinks of evolution merely as "change." Of course *some*
change occurs by natural process, so he reasons that therefore *all*

change must occur by natural processes. Because some variations are beneficial to the organism that possesses them—he cites the standard examples such as bacterial resistance to penicillin and insect resistance to pesticides—Miller thinks he has proved that a similar process of variation and natural selection can create new kinds of organisms with new complex organs. And because the fossil record indicates a history of variation within limits, he thinks he has proved that there are no limits to variation. No wonder Miller concludes that anybody who questions the Darwinian story must be as irrational as the mystic who denies that the 587.6 nanometer emission peak in the solar atmosphere signals the presence of helium!

Miller makes his fossil case by using the example of elephants. He begins by noting that "The skulls, teeth and jaws of elephants are distinctly different from other mammals, which makes extinct elephantlike organisms easily recognizable from fossils." Passing over the mystery of how this basic elephant type came into existence in the first place, Miller reports that there are two living elephant species—the African and Indian elephants—and a number of extinct variations on the basic form. He then says, "I can imagine Phillip Johnson . . . telling me with a straight face" that each of these variations was separately designed, and that "the sequence of their appearances is a misleading coincidence."[6] The argument embodies Miller's typical methodology: first he creates a straw man, then he ridicules it. The real Phillip Johnson would say that elephant variation is yet another example of the pervasive pattern that we see both in the fossil record and in the living world. Variation and diversification occur, probably to a greater extent in the remote past than in the present, but only within the confines of the basic type. There is no scientific explanation for the origin of that easily recognizable elephant type other than speculation based on unjustified extrapolation.

Even if the basic type did "evolve" (in some sense of that vague term) from some very different predecessor, and ultimately from a single-celled organism like a bacterium, we do not know any mechanism capable of producing such an amazing set of transformations.

Exactly how much natural variation and diversification *has* occurred would be a fruitful question for scientists to address if they were able to do so. Such investigation cannot occur, however, if scientists are incapable of anything more sophisticated than Miller's "all or nothing" way of defining the issue. Miller insists that "If evolution is genuinely wrong, then we should not be able to find *any* examples of evolutionary change *anywhere* in the fossil record."[7] To say that a proposition as broad and vague as "evolution" must be either completely right or completely wrong is to rule out any intelligent discussion of the subject. Of course evolution has occurred, if evolution simply means *change of any degree or kind,* and so in that trivial sense evolution is necessarily "right." But evolution is a much more dubious concept if it means *massive increases in genetic information produced by chance variation and differential reproductive success.* By that definition, evolution is very wrong.

Miller's incomprehension of the information problem is particularly visible when he turns to embryonic development. He says that no intelligent design theorists—who, for maximum pejorative impact, he calls creationists—"would reject the proposition that a single fertilized egg cell—the classic specimen of developmental biology—contains the full and complete set of instructions to transform itself into a complex multicellular organism. Neither would any respectable creationist challenge the assertion that every step of that developmental process is ultimately explicable in terms of the material processes of chemistry and physics. Miracles aren't required—the complexities of molecular biology will do just fine."[8] That is correct. Miracles are *not* required, but an intelligent cause *is* required. Instructions in the fertilized egg control embryonic development from the beginning and direct it to a specific outcome. This "full and complete set of instructions" *employs* the material processes of chemistry and physics but is not *created by* those processes. Similarly, the software in a computer employs natural processes to generate a word processing document, but the software has to be written by an intelligent agent. The relevant question is not whether miracles are required once the instructions are in operation but whether intelligence was required to create the instructions in the first place.

Miracles and design are distinct concepts. The resurrection of Jesus is a miracle, which means that it is an exception to the otherwise universal process of irreversible decay following death. When we ask whether design is present in biology, we are not asking about *exceptions* to normal processes but rather about what the normal process itself must have been. The issue is whether scientific evidence indicates that law and chance alone can accomplish biological creation or that an intelligence cause is also required. Musicians do not violate natural laws when they compose symphonies or perform on instruments, but they do add something to the laws without which music would not exist. Similarly, the genetic information does not violate any laws when it directs the development of the embryo in the womb, but it adds something to the laws without which development would not occur. It is the origin of that "something" that intelligent design theorists want to consider and that materialists want to rule out of consideration as "a question only a creationist would ask." The design position is falsifiable, since advocates of naturalism could discover a natural process capable of creating the necessary information if such a process exists. (If neo-Darwinism were true as a general theory of biological creation, it would falsify our claim that some additional information-creating mechanism is necessary.) The "design is religion, not science" position is not falsifiable because it decides the disputed question by the manipulation of words rather than by empirical investigation. *Hence, by the standard of falsifiability the intelligent design hypothesis is scientific, and the refusal to consider it on its merits is unscientific.*

Another Darwinist Responds: Robert Pennock

Robert Pennock at least acknowledges the problem of information creation but succeeds only in showing that he does not understand it. As I explained in chapter two, Pennock thinks that a computer creates new complex information when it "selects" the correct letters from a random array to match a target sentence by comparing them with a copy of the desired sequence which a programmer has written into its memory. Of course, both the selection program and the target text itself are products of intelligent design. The error is elementary, but it is one that countless Darwinists continue to make. Because they do not understand the difference between intelligent and unintelligent causes, they assume that unintelligent causes can do everything that intelligence can do—and maybe even more! Responding to my argument that unintelligent processes cannot create life, Pennock crows triumphantly that "so far we do not have a single case of intelligent creation of life; rather, our universal experience to date is that *only* unintelligent material processes do so."[9] Any logician would call that begging the question and also running away from the obvious. If human intelligence is incapable of creating life, then the logical inference is that a greater-than-human intelligence is required, not that inanimate matter can do the job on its own.

Pennock's main line of attack, however, is indicated by the title of his book *Tower of Babel*. He points out uncontroversially that a kind of evolution occurs in languages, so that (for example) both French and Spanish have gradually evolved from Latin. Exactly how far back this process of language evolution can be carried is unknown or disputed, but for convenience we may go along with Pennock's speculation that perhaps it can be extrapolated to a single initial language (now extinct) from which all the others developed.[10] A single origin of language would be comparable to the standard scientific assumption that all of today's organisms evolved through a chain of extinct ancestors from a single first replicator which emerged from a chemical soup. Pennock uses this example to make two points: first, the Tower of Babel story in Genesis is wrong because languages evolved gradually rather than being specially created with the fall of the Tower; second, objections to biological evolution made by persons such as Behe and Johnson must be insubstantial because they can be overcome in the case of linguistic evolution.

Pennock's argument from analogy actually tends to prove the opposite of what he intends. In the first place, intelligent design advocates (the "new creationists" targeted in Pennock's subtitle) do not bring Genesis into the discussion at all and hence claim no stake in the Tower of Babel story. That makes the whole argument irrelevant. But not to spoil the fun, let's suppose we did want to defend the story as history. In that case we would be delighted to discover that all modern languages evolved over time from a single original universal language, because the story relates that God "confused their language"—*not* that God created a bunch of utterly dissimilar languages from scratch. One would therefore expect that clues to the existence of the original common language might be found in the products of the confusion. The most impressive clue I can imagine would be a universal grammar, itself of mysterious origin, which underlies and governs all the superficially diverse languages that have evolved since humans first began to speak.

Ironically, the very enthusiastic Darwinist Steven Pinker uses the

Babel story to illustrate how diverse human languages could arise within the boundaries of the universal grammar that actually does characterize all of them. "God did not have to do much to confound the language of Noah's descendants," says Pinker. "In addition to vocabulary—whether the word for 'mouse' is *mouse* or *souris*—a few properties of language are simply not specified in the Universal Grammar and can vary as parameters. . . . There seems to be a common plan of syntactic, morphological, and phonological rules and principles, with a small set of varying parameters, like a checklist of options. Once set, a parameter can have far-reaching changes on the superficial appearance of the language."[11] Pinker observes that the "Universal Grammar is like an archetypal body plan found across vast numbers of animals in a phylum."[12] The archetype itself does not evolve, and succeeding generations of humans employ it without needing to be taught. If isolated groups of people invent new languages, their inventions will always be variations on the basic pattern that is common to all language.

In other words, language evolution is very much like the kind of biological evolution that scientists actually observe in that it occurs within the boundaries of an unchanging type that is itself of unknown origin. As with observed biological evolution, language evolution involves no increase in complex information or invention of new capabilities. It is precisely the fact that primitive languages are as complex as modern ones that first led linguistic scholars to the discovery that spoken language is the product of a special and uniquely human instinct, rather than a cultural invention like writing or agriculture. As Pinker puts it, "There are Stone Age societies, but no Stone Age language."[13] Evolution that takes the form of variation within the type without the creation of any new capability is entirely consistent with the proposition that intelligence was required to create the language instinct itself with its universal grammar. To use the vocabulary previously suggested, language evolution is horizontal, and it provides no explanation for the vertical leaps. If Pennock had wanted to cite a genuine analogy in language to vertical evolution in biology, he might have chosen the invention of the alphabet or arabic numerals. Only a creative intelligence could have invented the alphabet, but subsequent changes in the form of the letters could easily result from copying errors or other accidents of history.

The human language capacity (with its universal grammar) is a particularly serious difficulty for Darwinists, because it seems to have arisen all at once in humans without any true animal predecessors. That is why the famous linguist Noam Chomsky, who is the furthest thing from a creationist, is notoriously skeptical of the ability of the Darwinian mechanism to explain the origin of the language instinct.[14] Pennock acknowledges this fact and likens the problem to the origin of life itself, which "remains largely a mystery," but then invokes methodological naturalism to disallow any inference of design for either of these unsolved problems. That is to decide the question by arbitrary fiat. The origin of life and the origin of the human language capability both required immense quantities of new genetic information, which could not be generated by any combination of law and chance. Materialists are welcome to prove that assertion wrong, but to do so they will have to demonstrate the existence of a mechanism that can generate the necessary information. Imposing rules that make materialism or naturalism unfalsifiable is authoritarian politics, not science.

The Culture War

Miller and Pennock make various other points based on similar confusions, but to go into more detail would exhaust the reader's patience without making any real contribution to understanding what the dispute is all about. Like the denunciations that scientists and journalists directed at the Kansas state board of education in the controversy reported in chapter three, the barrage of rhetorical missiles is an offensive in a culture war rather than a serious attempt to grapple with the scientific issues. The essential conflict does not turn on evidentiary details, but on fundamentally opposed ways of thinking. If you accept and internalize the logic of scientific naturalism, then naturalistic evolution in some form will probably seem so obviously true that you will have trouble imagining how any well-informed, rational person can doubt it. You will ask not "Is there something wrong with evolution?" but "What hidden motive do these people have for denying the obvious?" That is why most elite scientists and intellectuals, including theistic modernists, do not even attempt to hold a reasoned discussion with their adversaries. Seeing themselves as embattled in a culture war against barbarians who want to return society to something like the Dark Ages, the defenders of scientific naturalism are extraordinarily undiscriminating about the arguments they employ. The strategy is to throw everything that comes to hand at the enemy in the hope that something will destroy this baffling, irrational menace.

Darwinists can take in stride any debates over the particulars of their theory, however strident, so long as the underlying principle of naturalistic explanation is not threatened. That is why the blatant heresies of Stephen Jay Gould, to take one example, were cheerfully tolerated until very recently. As John Maynard Smith, the British dean of Darwinists, famously summed up the professional judgment after Gould finally pushed the envelope too far, "The evolutionary biologists with whom I have discussed [Gould's] work tend to see him as a man whose ideas are so confused as to be hardly worth bothering with, but as one who should not be publicly criticized because he is at least on our side against the creationists." Gould's anguished response went to exactly the same point: "We will not win this most important of all battles [against the creationists] if we descend to the same tactics of backbiting and anathematization that characterize our true opponents." Everything is negotiable except the vital objective of keeping God out of objective reality. As Gould's ally Richard Lewontin put it, "we cannot allow a Divine Foot in the door. . . . To appeal to an omnipotent deity is to allow that at any moment the regularities of nature may be ruptured, that miracles may happen." In the materialist mentality, the appearance of the Lawgiver is equated with the disappearance of the laws.[15]

Heresy within the confines of the scientific community is one thing. The same heresy in the context of a popular revolt against scientific authority becomes an intolerable threat. When the Kansas state school board picked up the idea, long associated with Gould, that there might be a difference in kind rather than merely in degree between micro- and macroevolution, Darwinists universally responded with vehement denunciations implying that no respectable scientist had ever considered such nonsense. Of course there have been many scientists who have doubted that a grand evolutionary mechanism could be extrapolated from modest evidence of cyclical variations within a fundamentally stable species. The difference was that the scientists were speculating within the boundaries of methodological naturalism, whereas the Kansas board members clearly wanted to insert the divine foot in the door. Once the foot is in the door it is hard to shut out the rest of the divine presence, not to speak of the millions of people who are gathered behind it.

The need to shut out that foot explains not only the barrage of poorly reasoned scientific arguments from the Darwinist camp but also the accompanying insistence that "evolution" and "religion" are in no way in conflict. When the Darwinists are worried about popular revolt, they tell the Darwinian story with a mildly theistic spin.

They realize that it is safer to allow God a shadowy existence in human subjectivity than to run the risk that this very threatening presence will burst into objective reality. That is when we hear the standard vague reassurances that "many people believe in both God and evolution," or that "science does not say that God does not exist," or that "science and religion are separate realms." That is also when modernist leaders of mainstream denominations come forward to denounce those "fundamentalists" who are bringing Christianity into disrepute by mindlessly opposing "scientific knowledge," such as the knowledge that mosquito populations evolve a resistance to DDT. Once the danger is past, the reassurances will be put back on the shelf, and we will again hear that a proper understanding of "evolution" requires us to recognize that humans are just another animal species which, like all the others, is an accidental product of a purposeless cosmos.

In the final analysis, it is not any specific scientific evidence that convinces me that Darwinism is a pseudoscience that will collapse once it becomes possible for critics to get a fair hearing. It is the way the Darwinists argue their case that makes it apparent that they are afraid to encounter the best arguments against their theory. A real science does not employ propaganda and legal barriers to prevent relevant questions from being asked, nor does it rely on enforcing rules of reasoning that allow no alternative to the official story. If the Darwinists had a good case to make, they would welcome the critics to an academic forum for open debate, and they would want to confront the best critical arguments rather than to caricature them as straw men. Instead they have chosen to rely on the dishonorable methods of power politics.

Is there an alternative to Darwinism? When Darwinists ask that question, they have in mind an alternative of the same kind, meaning a new scientific explanation that involves only law and chance. In that sense, I doubt that there is an alternative. Many persons have tried to find such a theory by postulating innovative macromutations (perhaps in the so-called *hox* genes that are common to many distinct groups) or vaguely-defined self-organizing systems or chaos theory or new laws of physics. None of this ever comes to anything more than unkept promises, which is why neo-Darwinism retains its status as the default position. If nature is all there is, and matter had to do its own creating, then there is every reason to believe that the Darwinian model is the best model we will ever have of how the job might have been done. To confirmed materialists and other persons who are bemused by the mystique of science, that means that the theory has to be accepted as true regardless of all the reasons to believe that it is false. To me it means that there is good reason to conclude that materialism is false and that we need to consider a different kind of explanation for the situation in which we find ourselves.

7

BUILDING A NEW
FOUNDATION FOR REASON

What If We Start with the WORD?

The Balconers and the Travelers

In his classic book *Knowing God* J. I. Packer employed an attractive metaphor to distinguish between two kinds of interest in theology. Imagine a Spanish-style house, he wrote, with a large open balcony on the second floor. The people on the balcony are watching some travelers setting out on a long journey on the road below. The "balconers" can overhear the travelers and chat with them about such things as whether they are on the right road, whether they have all the right equipment and whether they ought to be undertaking this particular journey in the first place. The balconers are onlookers, and their concerns are theoretical. The travelers, in contrast, have made up their minds about where they want to go and how they are going to get there. They want to know how to overcome the obstacles before them, and they will probably be impatient if the balconers emphasize the difficulties in an unhelpful way.

Packer used the balcony metaphor to distinguish between theoretical and practical problems of Christian theology.[1] At the theoretical level, for example, there is the perennial question of whether the existence of evil and suffering can be reconciled with God's goodness and omnipotence. At the practical level, the Christian traveler wants to know how to overcome evil and bring goodness out of it. At the theoretical level, theologians debate the rationality of the doctrine of original sin. Christian travelers, knowing the reality of sin from within, want rather to know how they can be saved from it. Each kind of inquiry is appropriate in its place, but of course the travelers will not reach their destination if they are on the wrong road because they have assumed the wrong answers to the theoretical questions.

The same distinction between broadly theoretical and practical concerns can be applied to any complex enterprise. With respect to scientific investigation of the history of life, for example, we can ask two different kinds of questions: first, "What is the purpose of this inquiry?" and second, "Having decided or assumed the purpose, how can we best achieve that purpose?" Restating the first question more specifically, it is "Should we consider only natural causes— law and chance—or should we be open to the possibility that intelligent (and therefore possibly supernatural) causes were also necessary for biological creation?" Scientific travelers, who have made up their minds to pursue a program of purely naturalistic explanation all the way, may find this balcony question uninteresting, inappropriate and even offensive. "We settled that long ago," they might say, "when we decided that science is committed *a priori* to explanations that involve only natural causes. We are making excellent progress toward our destination, and meddling onlookers who wish to distract us are a nuisance."

That is exactly how the travelers of evolutionary science do respond. They have decided on their destination and the means they intend to employ to get there. Their plan is accurately described by the molecular biologist Richard Dickerson, in explaining why any reference to intelligent causes has to be rigorously excluded from biology:

> Science, fundamentally, is a game. It is a game with one overriding and defining rule: Rule No. 1: Let us see how far and to what extent we can explain the behavior of the physical and material universe in terms of purely physical and material causes, without invoking the supernatural.[2]

Up to a point this traveler-talk is legitimate. If you want to see how far you can go strictly on the basis of natural (or unintelligent) causes, then it makes sense to assume at first that you can go all the way. Any other assumption might lead to giving up on the project too soon, when the difficulties can still be overcome. On the other hand, the same logic implies that at some point you should stop to evaluate, and to do that you feel is necessary to suspend the assumption that everything can be ultimately explained as a product of law and chance. Maybe the naturalistic research project, however successful it may have been in explaining *some* things, is no good at all at explaining *other* things. To put it simply, you can't rationally decide whether you are on the right road unless you are willing to consider the possibility that you are on the wrong road.

Summing Up

The preceding chapters of this book have been aimed at explaining why the travelers need to return to the balcony for a discussion about basic principles. I began in the introduction with the starting point of the Wedge program: the crack between the two definitions of science. On the one hand, science means a practice of impartial empirical investigation and testing. On the other hand, science means a very partisan adherence to a philosophy variously called naturalism, materialism or physicalism. Refusing to recognize that there could be a difference between these two definitions is at the very heart of the philosophy of scientific naturalism. My hypothesis was that the Darwinian theory and its accompanying definition of knowledge will collapse once the difference is recognized, with profound consequences for the life of the mind.

The story of Philip Wentworth told in chapter one showed how overpowering naturalistic philosophy has been in the twentieth century, coming as it does with all the authority of "science," and how easily aspiring young intellectuals have been indoctrinated to think that naturalism and rationality are virtually the same thing. Wentworth's story also illustrated the related concept that reason (by naturalistic definition) is merely instrumental. Instrumental reason can tell us how to get more of whatever it is that we happen to want, but it can't tell us what we ought to want. It could hardly be otherwise if reason must draw everything from a starting point of matter in motion, because matter knows nothing of purposes or ultimate ends. We saw how Wentworth read this understanding of reason back into his childhood religious training, defining prayer as a magical means to get whatever we want rather than as a means to conform our rebellious wills to God's will. Judging by that standard, it is not surprising that he found science to be a more reliable way of getting what he wanted.

Chapter two addressed the question of complex genetic information, and whether Darwinian science has found an information-creating mechanism. The lesson of that chapter is encapsulated in Richard Dawkins's reaction to a request for proof that such a mechanism exists. Dawkins huffed that "it is a question that nobody except a creationist would ask." You can't get much more unscientific than that, because in real science a demand for evidence is always in order. Dawkins is willing to talk only to people who agree to *assume* that the information comes from some natural source—mutation, nonrandom death, or wherever. Dawkins is a traveler, and so is Paul Davies, although Davies seems close to recognizing that our current science lacks the concepts which would be required to account for the kind of information we find in living organisms.

Chapter three described what is basically the same argument but in the form of a cultural conflict over the teaching of evolution in the public schools of Kansas. The Kansas revolt and similar incidents in other states stem from public resistance to the campaign by science educators to insinuate metaphysical naturalism into the curriculum under the rubric of "the fact of evolution." The citizens who protest the policy of the science educators perceive correctly that the educators want to teach their children that naturalism is a fundamental truth for all purposes, not just a convention employed for limited purposes by professional scientists. The intellectual elites respond to their protest with the disreputable weapons of culture war: distortion, obfuscation, propaganda and intimidation. A genuine debate or conversation about the issues cannot occur, because the elites assume that it is futile to attempt to reason with any person who does not accept naturalistic metaphysics.

From time to time educational leaders contemplate starting a new kind of educational program to prepare science students to debate the issues in public. Such a program would be a disaster for the Darwinists if it ever got off the ground because you can't teach students to argue a case competently without familiarizing them with the best arguments on the other side. To refute Michael Behe and William Dembski the students would have to study their books, and in the process they would learn about irreducible complexity and the nature of complex specified genetic information. The students would also need to learn about such things as the defects in the peppered moth story, the fraud in the Haeckel embryo drawings, the mystery of the Cambrian explosion and what the leading Darwinists really believe about the implications of Darwinism for religion.[3] Before this education went very far, the authorities would have a mutiny on their hands. The Darwinists cannot change their tactics because any true education in evolution would cast the clear light of analysis on assumptions that cannot survive it.

Chapter four addressed the role of religion in this cultural conflict. By any realistic definition naturalism *is* a religion, and an extremely dogmatic one. It rests on a basic conviction about ultimate reality that is held by a kind of faith, and it incorporates its own definitions of "knowledge" and "reason." It says that knowledge comes ultimately from our senses and that the more complex forms of knowledge come from scientific investigation. By naturalistic definition there can be no such thing as *knowledge* of the supernatural. Statements about God are either *non*rational (if frankly presented as mere subjective belief) or *ir*rational (if they purport to make objective factual claims). This system of categories allows the metaphysical naturalists to mollify the potentially troublesome religious people by assuring them that science does not rule out "religious belief" (so long as it does not pretend to be knowledge). Relegating God to the realm of subjective belief is as attractive to some modernist theologians as it is to agnostics because it allows them to achieve a convenient reconciliation of Christianity with naturalism. The cognitive territory allowed for theology is so evanescent, however, that the philosophical rules have to be kept vague. If the theological modernists were to concede that they have no access to knowledge, then they would forfeit any claim to a teaching authority. On the other hand, if the scientific naturalists were to concede that the theologians actually have any cognitive status, then *they* would risk allowing the dangerous divine foot in the doorway. Keeping the peace on these "now you see it, now you don't" terms requires covering the subject with a fog of obscurity.

Chapter five explains why naturalism is ultimately incompatible with the existence of reason. I have told many lecture audiences that Darwinian evolution simply *must* be unguided because the purpose of Darwinism is to explain creation without allowing any role to God. On materialist assumptions there can be no mind to guide evolution until mind evolves mindlessly from matter. That is a true description of Darwinism as far as it goes, but there is more to be said. The logic of naturalistic reduction does not even stop at the appearance of the mind because the mind itself must ultimately be explainable in terms of unintelligent processes, whether these are firing neurons, replicating memes or whatever. One can try to stop the reductionist program by arbitrary fiat, as does the philosopher John Searle, but that is no more effective in quenching reductionist ambitions than the pope's insistence that the scientists treat the soul as an impenetrable mystery and leave it to the church. If mind came from matter *and nothing else,* then it must in principle be possible to explain mental processes in terms of physical processes, however far from doing so we may be at the present time. From a materialist perspective, to refuse to concede this reflects merely a failure of nerve. On the other hand, the logic of materialist reductionism implies that science itself is the product of unreasoning material causes. No wonder the Age of Reason ends with the age of postmodernist relativism! And yet we still see the reductionists complacently describing religious belief either as a meme or as the product of a "God module" in the brain without realizing that they are sawing off the limb on which they themselves are sitting. If unthinking matter causes the thoughts the materialists *don't* like, then what causes the thoughts they *do* like?

Finally, in chapter six we saw how academic Darwinists respond to these challenges, mainly with caricature, argumentative definitions, evasion of crucial difficulties like the information problem, and appeals to prejudice. I illustrated these tactics with two recent books that typify the range of Darwinian arguments. I have had many conversations with leading scientists, journalists and other intellectuals who are committed to evolutionary naturalism, as well as with theological modernists who express fundamentally naturalistic ideas in theistic language. When I refuse to accept naturalistic assumptions some are overtly hostile, some are patronizing, and some try their best to be polite. All are uncomprehending. To them naturalism and science are virtually the same thing, and they think that to depart from science is to depart from reason.[4]

A Balcony Conversation Between Religion and Science

If the situation is as I have described it, the intellectual bankruptcy of Darwinism cannot be concealed for very much longer. The Darwinists may delay the day of reckoning for a while by wielding the weapons of power, but more and more people are learning to press the right questions and to refuse to take bluff or evasion for an answer. By appealing to the scientific community's own standards of skepticism and objectivity they will eventually gain a hearing. Consequently I expect that fairly early in the new century a conversation between religion and science will occur on very different terms from the ones described in chapter four. It will be a "balcony conversation" because it will start when enough people realize that the travelers have been on the wrong road.

The old dialogue was concerned with whether religion deserves to retain *any* cognitive territory in a culture dominated by scientific reasoning, which of course meant naturalistic reasoning. In the new dialogue the religious people will have a lot more to say, and they will say it because they have *knowledge* which can help explain what has gone wrong in science. They will say that some influential scientists have committed the very error that they accused the religious people of committing. These scientists have believed what they wanted to believe, instead of listening to what their own evidence was trying to tell them. In time a substantial body of scientists will emerge whose first loyalty is to following the evidence rather than to defending a philosophy, and they will admit that Darwinism's authority rested on philosophical preference rather than unbiased testing. The new dialogue will center on the question "Why were so many intelligent people so confused for so long?"

One of the participants in that new conversation will be Christian theology. Of course there will be other participants as well, some of them scientific and some representing other religious traditions. We can't anticipate everything that they may say, but I can at least begin the conversation by sketching what I think the distinctively Christian voice *should* be saying. Evolutionary science has made many attempts to explain religion in general, or Christianity in particular, on naturalistic assumptions. Now it is time to return the favor, by allowing theology to explain why science is so reliable in some ways, and so disappointing in others, and why Darwinian science in particular has come to such a dead end. The place to begin is with the Biblical passage that is most relevant to the evolution controversy. It is not in Genesis; rather, it is the opening of the Gospel of John.

> In the beginning was the Word, and the Word was with God, and the Word was God. He was in the beginning with God; all things were made through him, and without him was not anything made that was made. (Jn 1:1-3 RSV)

These simple words make a fundamental statement that is directly contradictory to the corresponding starting point of scientific materialism. Using the Greek word *logos,* the passage declares that in the beginning there was intelligence, wisdom and communication. Moreover, this Word is not merely a thing or a concept but a *personal being.* This is important because only persons have purposes and make choices. If a personal entity is at the foundation of reality, then we have a secure basis for discussing what the world is *for* rather than merely the material means by which it works. This starting point also implies that there is more than one way of pursuing knowledge. If only things existed, then scientific investigation might be the only road to knowledge, but if the foundation of reality is personal, then there are other ways of knowing. We can learn about *things* only by studying them, but with *persons* we can also communicate. A personal being who is the Word at the foundation of reality can communicate with us in many ways. These include not only religious activities such as Scripture reading and prayer, but also literature, music, art and mathematics. People intuitively sense that great artists like Dante, Shakespeare, Bach and Rembrandt bring us something like glimpses of the nature of the divine mind, something that can never be understood within a materialist framework that sees all human activity as derived from the physical needs of survival and reproduction. Scientists marvel that mathematics is so surprisingly insightful in describing the physical cosmos, often in ways that the mathematicians who developed the theories could never have predicted. Reality is simply too rational and beautiful ever to be forced into the narrow categories that materialism can comprehend.

That God created us is part of God's general revelation to humanity, built into the fabric of creation. This foundational truth is something which, in the words of the political philosopher (and Wedge member) J. Budziszewski, *we can't not know.*[5] At a fundamental level we know the reality of God, and yet we often deny it. In another foundational biblical passage, the apostle Paul informs us that "what can be known about God is plain to [all people], because God has shown it to them." Paul continues:

> Ever since the creation of the world his invisible nature, namely, his eternal power and deity, has been clearly perceived in the things that have been made. So they are without excuse; for although they knew God they did not honor him as God or give thanks to him, but they became futile in their thinking and their senseless minds were darkened. Claiming to be wise, they became fools, and exchanged the glory of the immortal God for images resembling mortal man or birds or animals or reptiles. (Romans 1:20-23 RSV)

Even scientific materialists unwittingly acknowledge the truth of that passage in the very terms of their denial. Richard Dawkins opens *The Blind Watchmaker* with the comment that "biology is the study of complicated things that give the appearance of having been designed for a purpose."[6] The equally atheistic Sir Francis Crick warns in his autobiography that "biologists must constantly keep in mind that what they see was not designed, but rather evolved."[7] Darwinian biologists must keep repeating that reminder to themselves because otherwise they might become conscious of the reality that is staring them in the face and trying to get their attention. General revelation is not necessarily inconsistent with evolution in some senses of the term—observed microevolution or other limited variation within the type, for example—but it does contradict Darwinian claims that nature had the power to do its own creating. Only the Word creates, although the living things the Word creates have a capacity to vary in response to differing environments. That is why no natural mechanism has been discovered for the creation of new complex genetic information. No such mechanism exists.

God created us. At one level that is a truth we can't not *know,* and at another level it is a truth that we repeatedly *deny.* At some time or another almost everybody does want to deny it, because once we admit that we know God, we have to admit that we do not honor him as God, because we have chosen to follow our own rebellious wills rather than to submit to God's will. In a word, this is what we call *sin,* and not one of us is free from its effects. So denial is always a temptation, and outright atheism is only the most superficial form of denial. The atheist is always thinking about the true God in order to deny him, but this only makes other people think about the same subject, with the inevitable result that what they "can't not know" is constantly before their vision.

A much more sophisticated way of denying God is to relegate him to some marginal territory like "religious belief," where we don't have to think about him at all. By denying the possibility that we can ever have knowledge of God, the agnostic is able to meet the entire subject with a shrug and the patronizing comment that he never interferes with the religious beliefs of people who need that sort of crutch. Another time-honored strategy is to domesticate God by substituting something we can control. This is called idolatry. Primitive tribes make idols of wood or clay. Sophisticated modern intellectuals make idols of their theories, still employing the word *God* (as in "Spinoza's God") but in such a way that it adds nothing to chance and the laws of nature. All who pursue this strategy are substituting the created thing for the creator, and this is the essence of idolatry.

These passages from John 1 and Romans 1 provide the metaphysical basis for a Christian understanding of both science and pseudoscience. By the Word, God created a rational and contingent cosmos, and he created human beings in his image. Partaking in some degree of the qualities of the divine mind, we can understand a great deal through patient investigation of what we can see. The proper metaphysical basis for science is not naturalism or materialism but the fact that the creator of the cosmos not only created an intelligible universe but also created the powers of reasoning which enable us to conduct scientific investigations. Personality—first God's and then ours—is logically and ontologically prior to matter, and so a science which is founded in reality will always remember the fundamental distinction between persons and things, and will never imagine that it can understand the former by methods which are appropriate only for the latter. True science will also remember that only some aspects of reality can be understood through observation and experiments, and so it will never aspire to such an absurdity as a "theory of everything," nor will it attempt to explain thought itself as a product of physical forces. In a word, it will practice the theological virtue called humility. When you find scientists insisting that there are no limits or demanding that all human thought must be restricted to scientific categories, you can be sure that you are in the presence of pseudoscience.

Pseudoscience has its origin in the sin of pride, which refuses to respect the limitations inherent in our status as both created and fallen beings. Motivated by the sinful wish to control everything, pseudoscience distorts reality to conform it to our desires. Materialism is the characteristic concept by which twentieth century pseudoscience has accomplished this. Instead of beginning with the Word, materialism begins at the opposite pole with matter in motion. To make the difference clear I sometimes employ a parody of the biblical story:

> In the beginning were the particles;
> And the particles became complex living stuff;
> And the stuff imagined God;
> But then discovered Evolution.

This materialist story counterfeits the authority of science in order to masquerade as an inference from scientific evidence, but it is actually based on idolatrous fantasy. For this reason the materialist story thrives only as long as it does not confront the biblical story directly. In a direct conflict, where the public perceives the issues clearly, the biblical story will eventually prevail over the materialist story. The reason is that the biblical story is grounded on the solid rock of the reality we can't not know, and the materialist story is grounded on the shifting sand of human ambition. The materialists begin with great confidence to build a great Tower of Babel on that sand, and for a time their momentum is unstoppable. But in the end reality asserts itself, and the pretensions of pseudoscience end in confusion. Claiming to be wise, they become fools.

That is my explanation. It is consistent with the scientific evidence (as Darwinism is not), but of course it goes beyond anything that science can prove. Creation is not a scientific hypothesis but a metaphysical idea akin to naturalism or materialism. It is not a specific item of knowledge but a foundational premise that makes it possible to attain knowledge. Materialism as a foundational premise encouraged investigation of material processes, with many impressive results. The price was great, however, because carried to its logical conclusion materialism undermines all nonscientific categories of knowledge. Eventually it even undermines the mind itself, and that is when it becomes inescapably necessary to find a better starting point.

I do not present the argument in this chapter as a dogma, but as the best explanation of the situation in which we find ourselves. Of course my argument is wrong if the Darwinian theory explains as much as its devotees claim, but the true test of the Darwinian theory will come when we are finally able to force a public debate on even terms. I have no doubt as to what the outcome of that debate will be. Despite their immense cultural power, the Darwinists cannot prevail unless they can control the rules of reasoning and keep the debate within an arena where adherence to naturalism is required for a ticket of admission. That is why the Darwinists reacted with such universal panic to the Kansas rebellion, why they cannot afford to let go of the advantages provided by the *Inherit the Wind* stereotype, and why they cannot mount a genuine educational program to teach even their own students how to defend the theory. Education is the last thing they can afford, but education will come whether they like it or not. That is why their theory is doomed, however much political power is summoned to its defense.

"Who Do You Say That I Am?"

There is one step remaining. The Enlightenment rationalists thought that it was safe to reject God because it seemed to them that human desires are basically rational, and so the human problem is simply to choose the most rational means to achieve the ends on which all reasonable people can agree. The religion that Philip Wentworth remembered being taught as a child also took ends for granted and dealt only with means, and so it was not a very long step for him to adopt the more thoroughly secularized rationalism offered by his teachers at Harvard. The Christian diagnosis, however, is that the more fundamental human problem has to do with ends rather than means. What do we exist *for,* and why should we not live for pleasure, or in order to kill as many other people as possible before committing suicide? We are not capable of resolving that predicament on our own, least of all by the unassisted power of reason, because our reasoning powers are the very means we employ to construct whatever idol we are currently worshiping. To what or whom can we turn for a new starting point?

A mere *concept* of God in the human mind is no help at all, as we saw in chapter four, because a God created by human philosophy is just another idol. What we need is for God himself to speak, to give us a secure foundation on which we can build. If God has not spoken, then we have no alternative to despair. If God has spoken, then we need to build on that foundation rather than try to fit what God has done into some framework that comes from human philosophy. So it is of the greatest importance that we ask the question: "Has God *done* something to give us a start in the right direction, or has he left us alone and on our own?"

When we have reached that point in our questioning, we will inevitably encounter the person of Jesus Christ, the one who has been declared the incarnate Word of God and through whom all things came into existence. This time *he* will be asking the question that is recorded in the Gospels: "Who do men say that I am?"[8] As long as naturalistic reasoning governs all inquiry, Jesus' question has little importance. If people bother to answer it at all, they probably respond with something like this: "What does it matter? Probably you were a wise teacher or a plausible mountebank who was deified many years after your death by your followers, but the details hardly matter. However admirable you may have been, you have long been dead and you could not even conceivably be the starting point we are looking for because the accidental events of history can never supply the timeless truths of reason. The question you pose is therefore of no consequence to science or philosophy, and that is why we no longer regard it as worth discussing."

By naturalistic standards there is hardly any other way to answer, which is why our educational planners consider it enormously important that school children learn about evolution but entirely unimportant whether they learn enough about Jesus to evaluate his claims. When the naturalistic understanding of reality finally crashes and burns, however, the great question Jesus posed will come again to the forefront of consciousness. Who should we say that he is? Is he the one who was to come, or should we look for another?

As a Christian I have answers to those questions, and of course other people will have different answers. The Wedge philosophy is that the important thing is to get the right questions on the table, and that task requires that we invite any and all answers for a fair hearing. For now my point is merely that a question which was long assumed to be off the table will become important again if the cultural debate over Darwinism and naturalism goes in the direction I am predicting. We are not talking about some mere revision of a particular scientific theory. *We are talking about a fatal flaw in our culture's creation myth, and therefore in the standard of reasoning that culture has applied to all questions of importance.* Once we learn that nature does not really do its own creating, and we are not really the products of mindless natural forces that care nothing about us, we will have to reexamine a great deal else. In particular, we will need to have a new discussion about the nature of *reason,* and how we tell reason from rationalization, and whether there is a rationality of value as well as a rationality of fact, and what we might mean by the true, the good and the beautiful. Upon what foundation should we build our theories about all these things? After seeing that trying to build everything on a foundation of matter has led us into a blind alley, we will have to look for something better. Once the question is put that way, Christians have an answer. Scientists as such do not, although many scientists as citizens may have a lot to contribute. If other faiths have different answers, let them be heard so we can give them serious consideration.

The Universal and the Tribal
Any idea which aims to be a competitor in the universal marketplace of ideas must have universal appeal, which means that it must not be a mere tribal belief system that appeals only to people who were

brought up in that specific tradition. Many modernists think that only science is capable of making a universal appeal because only science is the same everywhere. Moral and social ideas differ enormously between China, Iran and the United States, but the principles for designing an airplane or a vaccine are the same in all three countries. Some social or moral ideas such as freedom of thought may be linked to the practice of science, and hence potentially universal, but from a naturalistic viewpoint ideas classified as "religious" are inherently tribal because they are based on subjective beliefs rather than objective reality. If that is the correct way to understand the subject, then Jesus must take his place among countless other religious teachers, possibly having some wisdom to contribute to the common store but in no way authoritative outside a cultural community of belief. The physicist Freeman Dyson took this position for granted in responding to John Polkinghorne's claim that science and theology have comparable cognitive status and comparable methodology. Dyson commented that he could not share Polkinghorne's vision because

> when all is said and done, science is about things and theology is about words. Things behave in the same way everywhere, but words do not. Quantum mechanics works equally in all countries and in all cultures. Quantum mechanics gives plants the power to turn the energy of sunlight into leaves and fruit, and it gives animals the power to turn the energy of sunlight into neural images in retinas and brains, whether they are living in Tokyo or in Timbuktu. Theology works in one culture alone. If you have not grown up in Polkinghorne's culture, where words such as "incarnation" and "trinity" have a profound meaning, you cannot share his vision.[9]

There is some truth in that paragraph, but it is greatly oversimplified. Matter in motion behaves the same way in all cultures, and that is why physicists can take in stride whatever challenges or misunderstandings they may encounter from religious leaders or philosophers. If we substitute psychology for physics as our example of "science," however, Dyson would probably agree that it is doubtful whether the theories of human behavior that are fashionable in New York or Vienna at any one time have any universal status. Some bodies of knowledge that we call "science" rest securely on repeatable experiments, mainly those that deal only with inanimate objects. Theories that deal with other kinds of entities tend to rely on agreement among the practitioners, and there we may find rival theories even within a single nation or ethnic group. This is true even of the most rigorous efforts to understand subjects that elude experimental confirmation, and of course it is especially true of pseudosciences such as Marxism, Freudianism and Darwinism. These may appear to have universal validity while they are at the height of their influence, but their hold on it is insecure. That is why Darwinists do *not* take challenges in stride but react in panic even to a narrow vote by a board of education in a minor state. Their authority rests on cultural power, and it will deflate as rapidly as the Leninist version of Marxism did if its adherents ever lose their power base.

Dyson also oversimplifies in the other direction, as we can see by comparing the two terms that he uses to categorize theology. The Trinity is a complex theological doctrine that causes notorious difficulties even for experts. Of course we would not introduce Christianity to African tribesmen or neglected slum children by reading them an academic treatise on the Trinity any more that we would introduce science education to the same people by giving them a lecture on the Copenhagen interpretation of quantum theory. The basic story of the incarnation—that God has taken human form and done something very important—is another matter altogether. It is more equivalent to the scientific truth that apples fall down rather than up, and it has enormous appeal to people from a variety of cultures who want something better than the idolatry they have been given. If Dyson supposes that the appeal of the Christian gospel is limited to a single culture, this merely shows how dated and provincial his own knowledge is. European and North American countries sent missionaries to Asia and Africa in the early twentieth century, to be sure. The process was unavoidably linked to Western economic and political imperialism, with the predictable backlash when the imperialists were replaced by independent national governments. That was then. Today many of the world's most vibrant Christian communities are in the postcolonial territories, and *they* are beginning to send missionaries to Europe and the United States to put new life in churches that have succumbed to modernism. If universal appeal is the standard, I would far rather be promoting the gospel of Christ around the world than the philosophy of the National Academy of Sciences.

To be eligible for consideration within a universal conversation, an idea (religious or otherwise) must be capable of being presented candidly to a critical audience with all the documents open for inspection and no assumptions concealed. This requirement is one of the great legacies of Enlightenment rationalism, and it necessarily limits the religious options that can qualify for consideration. A religious tradition that relies on protecting its founding documents from critical analysis or (much worse) that perpetuates itself by using violence to prevent its members from converting to another faith is not a competitor in the universal marketplace of ideas.

Enlightenment rationalism was essentially parasitic on Christianity because it provided no alternative foundation on which reason could build. It performed a great service to the Christian gospel, however, by forcing all Christian claims of authority to submit to the most rigorous and skeptical standards of critical inquiry. After two centuries of naturalistic science, accompanied by naturalistic theories of textual interpretation, it is Enlightenment rationalism that is feeling the pressure and dissolving into its antagonistic positivist and relativist components. The gospel of Christ is emerging from the trial with renewed strength. Certainly competing visions are welcome to participate in the great conversation that will occur after the fall of evolutionary naturalism, but I suspect there will be very few that can afford to pay the price.

8

TECHNOLOGICAL OPTIMISM
& LITERARY DESPAIR

How Can We Repair the Split in Knowledge?

Keeping God off the Table

My Berkeley colleague John Searle, who appeared previously in chapter five, is in some respects the very model of a modern monist materialist. In his latest book, which sums up the ideas that have made him fabulously successful in academia, Searle explains in his customary no-nonsense way why intellectual discussion in our time has gone "beyond atheism." He observes that materialists of previous generations (like John Stuart Mill and Bertrand Russell) thought they had to devote effort to refuting traditional theism. That is no longer necessary, says Searle, although the "religious urge" is as strong as ever in the general population. What has changed in our day is that "we no longer take the mysteries we see in the world as expressions of supernatural meaning. . . . Odd occurrences are just occurrences we do not understand." The definition of knowledge that dominates academia has changed to such an extent that it makes naturalism true regardless of the facts.

The result of this demystification is that we have gone beyond atheism to the point where the issue no longer matters in the way it did to earlier generations. For us, if it should turn out that God exists, that would have to be a fact of nature like any other. . . . If the supernatural existed, it too would have to be natural.[1]

Searle's "we" refers to the academic trendsetters, the kind of professors who carry the most influence in the leading universities and establish the ideas that reach the public via the mainstream media. That everyone may not think exactly as "we" do is barely recognized. This mode of writing is itself evidence of the philosophical narrowness that characterizes the academic elite. The really radical conclusion that follows from this way of defining knowledge is not so much that God doesn't exist but that it wouldn't matter to "us" even if he did exist. The conclusion is merely a refinement of what Philip Wentworth learned at Harvard in the 1920s: "All things, it seemed, were subject to the laws of nature. . . . In such an orderly universe there seemed to be no place for a wonder-working God. He would be an outlaw, unthinkable and impossible." Even if God existed he would be outside the ruling definition of knowledge and hence unworthy of notice. The rulers of knowledge are so puffed up with pride they imagine that even God is subject to their rules.

If theology is to say something worth hearing, it has to know something important that science has overlooked or denied for irrational reasons. Traditional Christian theology has some very good and very important knowledge to contribute, namely the gospel. "In the beginning was the Word" qualifies as important news, and "the Word became flesh and dwelt among us" qualifies as spectacularly important good news. Of course it is not good news unless it is true news, but the first point I need to make is that the news is important if it *is* true. The most effective argument that the most intelligent materialists make against Christian theism is not that they know the gospel to be false but that they know that it is safe to disregard the gospel whether it is true or false. This keeps the issue of true or false off the table. Their confidence comes from their embrace of a naturalistic understanding of knowledge. Science can provide knowledge because it relies on methods that are, in principle, open to everyone, although in practice you need a research grant to be able to do research. Moreover these methods have been so successful, the scientific naturalists claim, that we must acknowledge that they provide everything we need to understand everything that is understandable. If scientific reasoning falls short of complete understanding, then we must be content with partial understanding, because God can add nothing to human thought—himself being a product of human thought. What about Jesus and that supposedly empty tomb? That is *at the very most* no more than a single event which scientific reasoning cannot explain. In the formula that modernists call "Lessing's ditch" and the apostle Paul knew as Greek philosophy, the contingent truths of history could never supply the universal truths of reason. The concept was already ancient when Paul told the Athenian intellectuals that he could give a specific name and context to the "unknown God" which they worshiped.

The Greeks of our day are still unconvinced, and no constructive conversation can occur unless Christians confront their presuppositions directly and without evasions like "Spinoza's God." For present purposes I assume that Christians have something of value to say to people about their personal and spiritual problems.[2] These are matters that scientific intellectuals usually relegate to the private sphere, where illusory beliefs are acceptable "if they work for you." My concern is with public intellectual matters, the stuff that is discussed in the best journals and the best universities. Concerning those subjects, as discussed in that kind of forum—do those of us who know God have something of substantial merit and importance to say to those who do *not* know him? Can we participate confidently in the marketplace of ideas? I have no need to argue that we should *prevail* in that market. Once we are admitted, the truth will speak for itself, but that can happen only if we possess a truth that is capable of speaking for itself.

Science: The Right Questions

Because "evolution" is customarily defined as a scientific theory, the Wedge program is often put in the same category. This categorization leads critics like Kenneth Miller to demand that I or other Wedge members produce a "different theory," meaning a different historical theory that answers the same questions that Darwinism answers. The demand reflects a fundamental misunderstanding. Evolutionary science has been trying to build a materialist model of biological creation. To do this the scientists have assumed that life is fundamentally matter in motion, and they have concentrated on explaining how the matter arrives (chemical evolution) and how it changes (chance and natural selection). There is nothing wrong with the model *per se*; it is probably the best that can be built on materialist assumptions. It is the assumptions that are wrong. The task for now is to provide not a better materialist model but a better set of assumptions that will lead science to discard the wrong questions and embrace the right questions.

If the evolutionary scientists were better informed or more scientific in their thinking, they would be asking about the origin of information. The materialists know this at some level, but they suppress their knowledge to protect their assumptions. Richard Dawkins states the problem eloquently at some times, for example, but then he mystifies his readers with nonsense like computer selection programs that already incorporate the information. If the scientists were to acknowledge the true character of the information that governs the life processes, they would have to admit that they do not know how a combination of chance and natural law could do the creating. That would require acknowledging that the existing theory of the history of life is at best radically incomplete and possibly altogether erroneous. Claiming to have knowledge is not a triumph for science unless it is true knowledge, and admitting that we don't have answers is an improvement on dogmatically retaining the wrong answers.

Some argue that such an acknowledgment would cripple scientific research, but this is also nonsense. The parts of biological science that are achieving real progress would be only modestly affected by the recognition that intelligent causes necessarily played a crucial role in biological creation. That is because they are only nominally committed to materialist assumptions. Biological technology already starts from the premise that it is studying a form of "engineering," which is to say that it is attempting to decide how to understand and modify design. Biochemists talk about the libraries of genetic information stored in DNA, and how RNA translates the four-letter language of nucleotides into the twenty-letter language of proteins, and how they can "reverse engineer" specific biochemical structures to determine what functions they perform. This is the language of intelligent design, and it will continue much as before when the Wedge program is generally accepted but with a better philosophical fit.

Technological Optimism and Literary Despair

The Wedge has important things to say about science, but it has much more important things to say about the nihilism that infects intellectual life outside of experimental science. Lesslie Newbigin, one of the wisest of contemporary theologians, describes our contemporary intellectual culture as combining "technological optimism and literary despair."[3] Technology is at the flood tide of rationalist optimism, whereas the fields we call "the humanities" are at the ebb tide of nihilism. The task for any new way of looking at the world is not to feed the already excessive technological optimism but to speak to the literary despair. Why do we no longer have a rational basis for distinguishing good literature or music from bad, and why do we no longer understand what the purpose of a liberal education could possibly be? Readers will recall that Philip Wentworth in 1932 warned that "our educators are so busy building new dormitories and thinking up new systems of instruction that they do not see how urgently the situation calls on them to redefine the purposes for which their pedagogical machinery exists." The science and engineering departments, along with the professional schools like law and medicine, are shielded from the full effects of the crisis to the extent that they purport to supply only instrumental knowledge. The same is not true for the literature and philosophy departments, which teach things that ordinarily provide no route to wealth or power. If those departments had to justify their continued existence, could they make a convincing case?

Alvin Kernan's autobiographical account of academic life, *In Plato's Cave*,[4] provides an engaging account of what we may call a revolution of constantly lowering expectations. Kernan, a much-decorated hero as an enlisted man in the World War II Navy, grew up in poverty in rural Wyoming and never would have gone to college except for the G.I. Bill.[5] He began his formal education in the humanities with the noblest of expectations:

> I was one of those who feel that the most satisfactory end in life is knowledge; not money or power or prestige, but an understanding of people and the world they inhabit. . . . I had in my innocence developed a view of knowledge that will seem laughable in our skeptical

days. Read the right books and listen to the right people, think in the most intense and logical fashion . . . and all the darkness of Plato's cave of illusions would burn away in the bright sun of understanding. I did not think that truth remained to be discovered; I believed that in the main it already had been found and that I just had not yet been informed of the results.[6]

Kernan went on to become a professor of English at Yale, provost of Yale University, and dean of the graduate school at Princeton. He was for many years a brilliant and popular teacher, also widely respected as a scholar and academic statesman. His academic career was successful far beyond anything he could have imagined as a schoolboy or Navy enlisted man, but his autobiography is nevertheless a catalog of disappointments. Many of the most visible students at the very best universities turned into fascists of the left in the political crises of the 1970s and into hedonistic philistines thereafter. The knowledge Kernan had sought either never existed or faded like a mirage as he tried to come near it. The English departments turned to the relativism of deconstruction and to a power politics so all pervasive that the ruling dictum was "read only until you find the victim."[7] By 1990 the universities were much wealthier, with a few academic superstars living like celebrities, but the humanities departments were no longer involved in a search for knowledge. Near the end of his career Kernan reflected that "it takes an effort to remember the bright hopes of discovering truth that made academic study so lively and so promising in the period after World War II. . . . The feeling of great achievement is gone now, almost without a trace, disappearing into its own impossibility. Relativism and politicization did not destroy it; they filled the vacuum when the old dreams of absolute truth and great learning failed, and the universities they now govern are fragmented, nervous, uncertain, demoralized."[8]

Promises, Promises

What failure of navigation produced this vacuum? Kernan concluded with the reflection that "the gyroscope at the center of any educational system . . . is its dominant conception of knowledge." Indeed it is, and this factor accounts both for the exaggerated optimism at mid-century and the despairing nihilism at the end of the century. Scientific naturalism was at its peak in the years just after World War II. The war was won by technologies like radar, sonar and code breaking. Atomic energy promised an unlimited cheap power supply, while vaccines, antibiotics and pesticides promised a virtual end to disease. Traditional religion lost its place in intellectual discussion, but hardly anyone perceived this as a loss. Varieties of secular or religious humanism promised to fill the vacant place, providing a basis for morals and for meaning in life without the "superstition." This failed promise left the vacuum that relativism and politicization filled.

Alvin Kernan came to Yale just when William F. Buckley's *God and Man at Yale* had created a sensation by (in Kernan's words) arguing "provocatively and brilliantly that the administration and faculty of Yale, despite Yale's having been founded on religion and being still supported by free enterprise, were systematically teaching atheism and socialism in the classroom." Kernan saw Buckley's attack merely as an incident in the anticommunist politics of the time and implicitly certified its truthfulness while dismissing it from serious consideration. Classroom ridicule of religion was merely harmless joking, he thought, and it was absurd to imagine that liberals could be violating the academic freedom of conservatives.

> But we children of the Depression, raised in the Age of Roosevelt, were so indoctrinated with liberal views that we took them as simply given and obvious truth. They *were* the truths that academic freedom

made it possible to teach. It never occurred to us to doubt that Hiss was innocent, that McCarthy was a total liar, that the state was the best means for remedying all evils; and so we joined with everyone else in reviling and laughing at Buckley.[9]

That was the "we" of mid-century, which was well on the way to becoming the "we" that regards God as uninteresting, something to joke about in class before we get to the really important business of how Caesar can remedy all evils. Because the Christian gospel was out of the picture, it was essential to substitute an optimistic picture of human nature for the unpleasant reality of original sin. Therefore, the model of knowledge at the best universities assumed that humanity's problems were due to ignorance and poverty, which could be remedied by education and benevolent social engineering. Science would provide the technology while the humanities provided the vision. Alas, the humanities very quickly ran out of vision.

The Beginning of Wisdom

Lesslie Newbigin traced the origin of the contemporary crisis back to the attempt of René Descartes in the seventeenth century to find a fresh starting point for thought. Descartes lived in a time of skepticism much like our own, when scientific discoveries had overturned knowledge that had been settled for centuries. Seeking a foundation of absolute certainty on which to build, Descartes famously found it in the thinking subject: "I think, therefore I am." He thought that this was the one premise that could resist all skepticism, since even our doubts are examples of thought. As summarized by Newbigin:

> From this starting point he moved to the idea of God—but a God who is essentially an implicate of the human idea of perfection, and to the material world which belongs to a totally different order of existence from the mind. In this dualistic world God could influence the human

mind, but he could not act upon the material world itself. Many writers have commented on the way in which Descartes' dualism has shaped the whole of our subsequent thinking, creating a dichotomy which runs right through our culture, a dichotomy represented on every university campus by the divide between the science faculty and the faculties of arts and humanities.[10]

The dichotomy is also manifest in policy statements such as Gould's NOMA proposal. The realm of the mind held its own against the realm of matter until the mid-twentieth century, when scientific triumphalism upset the balance. Although formally the two realms may seem to have equivalent status, the dominance of the scientific naturalist definition of knowledge eventually ensures that no independent source of knowledge will be recognized. For the same reason that the realm of theology turned out to be empty in mid-century, in later decades the realm of the humanities turned out to be built around a vacuum. Even the one thing Descartes was sure that nobody could doubt—the existence of the thinking subject—is at the end of the century very much in doubt, as we saw in chapter five. It is no wonder that literary scholars filled the knowledge vacuum with the doctrine that writing is a kind of technology, the art of using words and symbols in the quest for power. After all, science teaches that life is merely a competition among genes seeking to maximize their own reproductive success. Given materialist premises, ideas can be judged objectively only on the basis of what interests they serve and how well they serve them.

Inevitably the same nihilism is at last being turned against science itself. One should be careful not to trivialize this tendency, as defenders of rationalism often do. Nobody really doubts such basic scientific truths as that apples fall down rather than up, and postmodernist relativists are as concerned as scientific rationalists that the airplanes on which they fly be designed and maintained according to scientific principles. Nobody, including religious fundamentalists and New Age gurus, doubts that scientific technology (like propaganda) is useful in the pursuit of wealth and power. Skepticism does not arise at that level, but it does become important when we get to broader considerations in subjects where there is no clear-cut experimental test to settle arguments. Anyone who reads about the controversies involving the nature of intelligence and its heritability, or whether "nature" designed males and females for different roles, or the details of the HIV theory of AIDS, or the various inflationary models of the big bang, knows that there is a lot of passionate disagreement in science. Moreover, the disagreements are not necessarily resolved in a process of open debate. There are political alliances, ideological commitments and differing degrees of influence in the peer review process that governs publication and funding. Perhaps most important, there are sometimes multibillion dollar financial interests at stake in what otherwise might look like ordinary scientific controversies. The struggle to prevail may seem like fairminded evaluation to the winners, but it often looks like power politics to the losers.

At times even science itself resembles a theater in which competitive genes go to battle wielding memes. In a nihilistic culture the rulers will wish to harness the technology of science for whatever ends they happen to prefer. The resulting regimes will not be tolerant, although they may employ the rhetoric of tolerance to discredit any notion that there can be knowledge in the realm of value. The absence of any rational basis for choice does not lead to tolerance. It leads to an unlimited struggle for power, specifically the power to enforce one's preferred standards of political correctness.

Scientists tend to be double-minded about how flexible science ought to be when confronted with critics of orthodoxy. On the one hand, they say that the glory of science is that it is never dogmatic, always open to revision and by nature tolerant of skepticism. These traits supposedly distinguish science from religion, which (in scientific circles) is assumed to be inherently dogmatic and obtuse. However, anyone who tries to take advantage of the implied invitation to be skeptical quickly learns that it has severe limits. You can question existing theories within the limits permitted by the professional community, and maybe you can doubt one important concept if you are sufficiently deferential. Try to challenge two ideas or one *really* fundamental idea and you will be met with a reaction I have learned to call *metaphysical panic*. The hands will shake, the voice will quaver, and you will be dismissed as an enemy of reason. This happens frequently to me in private; we saw its public manifestation in chapter three. Such panic is only to be expected. In the eyes of scientific rationalists, critics who go too far are threatening to return the world to that intolerable regime of skepticism from which the successors of Descartes have supposedly redeemed us.

Newbigin brings to theology a truth that the chemist and philosopher Michael Polanyi derived from science. There is no automatic road to objectivity, no talisman that can exempt us from taking personal responsibility for the fundamental propositions on which we build. As a legal scholar, I know this is true of constitutional law or any other kind of law. A certain kind of idealist longs to save humanity by giving it a written constitution that will protect the liberty of the individual and the local community even if the national government is taken over by scoundrels. This haven is a fool's paradise because eventually the task of interpreting the written constitution will also be taken over by scoundrels, or at least by persons who think that the constitution has to be brought up to date, to incorporate what "we" have decided to believe. The dream of escaping from subjectivity by positing a thinking subject or a rule of scientists or Supreme Court justices as philosopher kings is equally chimerical.

When the scientists, philosophers and judges see that they have the philosopher's stone under their own control, they will write their own ideologies into the definition of reason. Of course, the same is true of church authorities. There is no mechanism that can automatically protect us from unreason.

That brings us to the ultimate point. Human reason is a wonderful instrument if it is grounded in reality, but the instrument is just as good for rationalizing as it is for reasoning. Reason cannot provide its own premises because its main tool is logic. Logic tells us how to get from premises to conclusions but not how to know which premises we can rely on. If we try to derive our ultimate premises by reasoning from other premises, as modernists have been taught to do, we only make ourselves captive to circular reasoning. If reason is to be a reliable guide, it must be grounded on a foundation that is more fundamental than logic and that provides a basis for reasoning to true conclusions about ends. Instrumental reason is not enough. That is why the fear of the Lord is not the beginning of superstition but the beginning of wisdom.

Notes

Chapter 1: Philip Wentworth Goes to Harvard
[1]Jaroslav Pelikan, *Jesus Through the Centuries: His Place in the History of Culture* (New Haven, Conn.: Yale University Press, 1985), p. 206.

Chapter 2: The Information Quandary
[1]Barry Williams, "Creationist Deception Exposed," *The Skeptic* 18, no. 3 (1998); also available on the Internet at <www.onthenet.com.au/~stear/creationistdeceptionexposed.htm>. This article seemed designed to give the impression that on the final videotape a different question was substituted for the one Dawkins was actually asked in the interview. It was clear from the tape itself that the question was stated on the finished videotape by a narrator in a studio, rather than by the on-the-scene interviewer who would have actually asked it, as is common in television documentaries. Williams wrote about how "it would be quite simple, technically, for the interviewer or tape editor to record a totally different set of questions and splice them together with the interviewee's answers, thus making the interviewee look like a complete idiot." He went on to say that this would be legitimate on a comedy program where no deception was intended, but then used the Australian video as an example of where such a substitution would be fraudulent. The Australian interviewer Gillian Brown responded indignantly to the insinuation that they had substituted another question, showing with the raw tapes that the long pause actually was in response to the question asked by the interviewer in Dawkins's home: "Professor Dawkins, can you give an example of a genetic mutation, or an evolutionary process, which can be seen to increase the information in the genome?" This was followed on the tape with the eleven-second pause, actually shorter than the pause on the raw tape, after which Dawkins answered: "There's a popular misunderstanding of evolution that says that fish turned into reptiles and reptiles turned into mammals and that somehow we ought to be able to look around the world today and look at our ancestors and see the intermediate species." Brown's response is published on the Internet at <http://www.answersingenesis.org/docs/3907.asp>. Williams answered by saying that "Ms. Brown's whole argument and her accusations against me of 'irresponsible journalism' seem to revolve around one central issue; that I had accused her of inserting a different question into the tape from the one asked of Dawkins. But that is not the case, and my charges against her and, more particularly, against Answers in Genesis (the organization that markets the tape) do not at all depend on the insertion of a different question. What they do depend on is a whole series of events and actions whose culmination is a distorted presentation of Richard Dawkins' position. I did not accuse her of inserting a dummy question, though I did canvas that proposition in general discussion of the many ways in which interviews can be manipulated" (see <www.onthenet.com.au/~stear/brownresponse.htm>).
[2]The Dawkins statement is included in Williams,"Creationist Deception Exposed," n. 1.
[3]Richard Dawkins, "The Information Challenge," *The Skeptic* 18, no. 4 (1998); available on the Internet at <www.onthenet.com.au/~stear/dawkinschallenge.htm>.
[4]For example, the U.S. National Academy of Science's official publication *Teaching About Evolution and the Nature of Science* (Annapolis: National Academy Press, 1998) defines

evolution as "change in the hereditary characteristics of groups of organisms over the course of generations. (Darwin referred to this process as 'descent with modification.')"

[5]See, e.g., Richard Dawkins, "Human Chauvinism: Review of *Full House* by Stephen Jay Gould," *Evolution* 51, no. 3 (1997); on the Internet at <www.world-of-dawkins.com/fullhouse.htm>.

[6]Jill Cooper, "A New Germ Theory," *The Atlantic*, February 1999.

[7]Lee Spetner, *Not by Chance! Shattering the Modern Theory of Evolution* (Brooklyn, N.Y.: Judaica Press, 1997-1998).

[8]Ibid., pp. 138-44.

[9]See, e.g., Paul Davies, *The Mind of God: The Scientific Basis for a Rational World* (New York: Simon & Schuster, 1992).

[10]Paul Davies, *The Fifth Miracle: The Search for the Origin of Life* (New York: Simon & Schuster, 1999).

[11]Ibid., p. 6.

[12]George Wald, "The Origin of Life," *Scientific American*, August 1954, pp. 44-53.

[13]Christian de Duve, *Vital Dust: Life as a Cosmic Imperative* (New York: BasicBooks, 1995).

[14]Davies, *Fifth Miracle*, pp. 210-16.

[15]Ibid., pp. 218-19.

[16]Clive Cookson, "Scientist Who Glimpsed God," *Financial Times*, April 29, 1995, p. 20.

[17]Davies, *Fifth Miracle*, p. 89.

[18]Robert Pennock, *Tower of Babel: The Evidence Against the New Creationism* (Cambridge, Mass.: Bradford, 1999), p. 259.

[19]Ibid., p. 261.

[20]Readers who already understand the computer selection fallacy may suppose that I am attacking a straw man that is put forward only by unsophisticated Darwinists. This is emphatically not the case. Implicit belief in the computer selection fallacy is widespread among Darwinists because it is essential to their belief that a law-chance combination can produce all the necessary genetic information. Those who (like Dawkins himself) appear to understand that it is a fallacy nonetheless encourage others to believe it. This fallacy under-lies all the efforts to support the Darwinist mechanism with purported computer simulations, which invariably smuggle intelligence into the solution in the form of the computer program and the designed boundary conditions.

See, for example, the unsigned review of Michael Behe's *Darwin's Black Box* in *The Skeptic* 4, no. 3 (1996); available on the Internet at <www.world-of-dawkins.com/box/skeptic.htm>. The review ends with this paragraph:

> The answer to these arguments (for intelligent design in biology) can be found in complexity theory. Complex Adaptive Systems learn as they grow. Genetic mutations are chancy, but natural selection and the evolution of complexity are not. Natural selection preserves the gains and eradicates the mistakes. A monkey randomly typing will never produce Hamlet; but a monkey that learns, or a computer system that holds all correctly sequenced letters and disregards the rest (a la natural selection), will peck out "TOBEORNOTTOBE" in a matter of minutes. Does this happen at the cellular level! It does. It happens at all levels, and Stuart Kauffman, in his book *The Origins of Order* (Oxford, 1993), shows how, as does Gould's *Full House*.

It is noteworthy that Pennock and other Darwinists still do not see the fallacy in the computer selection model even after it has been pointed out to them. Pennock explains that

"Dawkins and Sober had *not* meant their examples as analogies for natural selection on random variation, but rather as illustrations of the power of *cumulative* selection on random variations, which is just the aspect of the Darwinian process that is relevant to the improbability argument" (Pennock, *Tower of Babel,* p. 261). This is semantic gibberish. Cumulative selection is just continuing natural selection, and it doesn't "select" any correct letters unless the computer is programmed with the target sequence. Try running the experiment again after erasing "methinks it is like a weasel" from the computer's memory, and you will be left with absolutely nothing but meaningless random combinations of letters and no progress whatever toward the target sentence. That leading Darwinists regularly make such an elementary logical error and obtusely persist in it after correction indicates the enormous mystifying power that an ideology can generate.

[21]The seminal work on testing the hypothesis of universal common descent is Paul Nelson, *On Common Descent,* University of Chicago Evolutionary Monographs 16 (Chicago: University of Chicago Press, 2000).

Chapter 3: The Kansas Controversy

[1]Hanna Rosin, "Creationism Evolves; Kansas Board Targets Darwin," *Washington Post,* August 8, 1999, p. A1. All quotations attributed to Hanna Rosin are from this article.

[2]The United States National Academy of Sciences officially adopted the "separate realms" formula in a 1981 policy statement. The Academy's 1984 booklet on *Science and Creationism* emphasized this approach in the preface by the Academy's president, Frank Press: "A great many religious leaders accept evolution on scientific grounds without relinquishing their belief in religious principles. As stated in a resolution by the Council of the National Academy of Sciences in 1981, however, 'Religion and science are separate and mutually exclusive realms of human thought whose presentation in the same context leads to misunderstanding of both scientific theory and religious belief.' " This statement continues to be quoted as authoritative by Academy representatives such as Dr. Bruce Alberts, the current president, although it can hardly be taken seriously. Leading members of the academy continually publish books and articles presenting science and religion in the same context mainly to promote the thesis that religion must yield to science on questions of fact and that "religious principles" are rational only to the extent that they implicitly abandon supernaturalism and at least tacitly embrace naturalism. This subject is addressed more fully in chapter four.

[3]The specific wording and word counts regarding the Kansas proposals were compiled by my associate Jonathan Wells from the original documents. The details are mainly of historical interest because the Kansas board of education had to revise the standards again after national science organizations denied permission to quote copyrighted material from the national standards.

[4]Stephen Jay Gould, "Is a New and General Theory of Evolution Emerging?" *Paleobiology* 6, no. 1: 119-30; reprinted in Maynard Smith, ed., *Evolution Now: A Century After Darwin* (Gordonsville, Va.: W. H. Freeman, 1982), pp. 129, 131. In this paper Gould envisaged "a potentially saltational origin for the essential features of key adaptations" (Smith, *Evolution Now,* p. 140). I discuss Gould's attempt to split the difference between Darwinism and saltationism in Phillip Johnson, *Darwin on Trial* (Downers Grove, Ill.: InterVarsity Press, 1993), pp. 40-41. I discuss Gould's overall ambivalence toward Darwinism in my essay "The Gor-

bachev of Darwinism," in *Objections Sustained* (Downers Grove, Ill.: InterVarsity Press, 1998).

[5]Brian Goodwin, preface to *How the Leopard Changed Its Spots: The Evolution of Complexity* (New York: Scribner's, 1996), pp. viii-ix.

[6]C. Mann, "Lynn Margulis: Science's Unruly Earth Mother," *Science*, 1991, pp. 252, 378-81.

[7]"Evolutionists have often protested 'unfair' to quoting an evolutionist as if he were against evolution itself. So let it be said from the outset that the vast majority of authorities quoted are themselves ardent believers in evolution. But that is precisely the point, and the value of *The Revised Quote Book*. The foundations of the evolutionary edifice are hardly likely to be shaken by a collection of quotes from the many scientists who are biblical creationists. In a court of law, an admission from a hostile witness is the most valuable. Quoting the evolutionary paleontologist who admits the absence of in-between forms, or the evolutionary biologist who admits the hopelessness of the mutation/selection mechanism, is perfectly legitimate if the admission is accurately represented in its own right, regardless of whether the rest of the article is full of hymns of praise to all the other aspects of evolution" (A. Snelling, *The Revised Quote Book* [Brisbane: Creation Science Foundation, 1990], inside cover). If a critic does *not* employ direct quotes from recognized Darwinian authorities when describing any part of the theory, he can expect the response that he is attacking a straw man, and that the theory is entirely different from whatever the critic has described.

[8]See Michael Behe, *Darwin's Black Box: The Biochemical Challenge to Evolution* (New York: Free Press, 1996). On the issue of quotations, Behe has commented: "[Jerry] Coyne complains [that *Darwin's Black Box*] is 'heavily larded' with quotations from evolutionists. This leads into his being upset with being quoted himself, as discussed above. That aside, however, I don't know what to make of this statement. What is a book concerning evolution supposed to contain if not quotes from evolutionists? Quotes from accountants?" (Behe, "Reply to My Critics," *Boston Review*, November 1996 [unarchived *Boston Review* Web discussion]).

[9]See William Dembski, *Intelligent Design: The Bridge Between Science & Theology* (Downers Grove, Ill.: InterVarsity Press, 1999); and *The Design Inference* (Cambridge: Cambridge University Press, 1998).

[10]My favorite of the commentaries that seems to have been written with the aid of a "bash creationism macro" was by Marianne Means of the Hearst chain in her column "Bush, Dole, Forbes Take Cover on Evolution," *Seattle Post-Intelligencer*, August 22, 1999, p. G2. Disappointed that the Republican candidates didn't take a strong stand for evolution and unaware that the front-running Democrat Gore was also about to waffle, she thundered her indignation:

> If our putative leaders don't believe in evolution, their know-nothing attitude in the White House could endanger our very national survival. If they do, their failure to defend it reflects a scary indifference toward education and our ability to compete in the high-tech, super-informed world of the next century. . . . In poll after poll, education ranks as the highest priority of American voters. A secular nation about to enter the 21st century requires the practical knowledge about the complexities of the universe that comes from scientific study. There is an important role for spiritual guidance in our church-going nation, but it must be complementary rather than supplementary. But Bush, Dole and Forbes didn't get it. They allowed as how they would let local officials determine what to tell young people about the origins of life rather than endorse the extensive paleontologi-

cal, biochemical, geographical and other factual evidence upon which the scientific community relies.

The three candidates are so intimated by the religious conservatives that they are not willing to contest the Kansas school board's suggestion that Charles Darwin was a jerk who held nutty, unverifiable theories no better than anyone else's.

What's next? Will our political heroes tell us they can't decide whether the Earth is flat or round? What if some school board somewhere declares Lucy, the famous 3.2 million-year-old Ethiopian mummy once admired by President Clinton, to be a fraud made of plastic?

A reader might wonder why if education is the highest priority of American voters, it is unsafe to leave curricular matters to officials elected by the voters to decide such questions. More amusing is that Means evidently doesn't know the difference between a fossil and a mummy, and appears to believe that President Clinton's admiring gaze has some authenticating power.

[11]Jonathan Weiner, "No Monkey Business," *Times Higher Education Supplement*, August 23, 1999.

[12]Maxine Singer, *Washington Post*, August 18, 1999, p. A19.

[13]Julia Keller, "Creative Tension: A Sister's Faith Can't Dispel Doubts About Suppressing Education in Kansas," *Chicago Tribune*, August 22, 1999, Perspective, p. 1.

[14]Philip Mathias, "That's Why It's Called the *Theory* of Evolution," *National Post of Canada*, August 19, 1999.

[15]Steve Kraske, "Creationism Evolves into Campaign Topic," *Kansas City Star*, September 3, 1999, p. A1. The Gallup poll of June 25-27 is also reported in the graph attached to the *New York Times* story by George Johnson, *infra.*, n. 10. This poll and related ones are posted at the Gallup Web site <www.gallup.com/poll/releases/pr990709.asp>.

[16]Editorial, "Darwin and the Candidates," *Washington Post*, August 30, 1999, p. A18. See also Hanna Rosin, "Gore Avoids Stance Against Creationism," *Washington Post*, August 27, 1999, p. A8. Rosin's first sentence is effectively sarcastic: "Vice President Gore, known for his love of science education, refused yesterday to take a clear stand on whether public schools should be required to teach evolution and not creationism." Of course representatives of the scientific community were enraged. Rosin quoted Berkeley biologist Daniel Koshland as saying, "It reflects badly on him that he would say something incorrect in order to appease all parts of the population." A presidential candidate can hardly be expected to thumb his nose at over two-thirds of the electorate, however.

[17]Robert E. Hemenway, "The Evolution of a Controversy in Kansas Shows Why Scientists Must Defend the Search for Truth," *Chronicle of Higher Education*, October 29, 1999; also found at <http://chronicle.com>.

[18]Phillip E. Johnson, "Counterpoint: The Religious Implications of Teaching Evolution," *Chronicle of Higher Education*, November 12, 1999; also found at <http://chronicle.com>. The title was chosen by the editors; I preferred my own title: "Why Not Teach the Controversy?"

[19]In March 2000, People for the American Way (PAW) published a public opinion poll on these issues. PAW is an enforcer of scientific naturalist orthodoxy and political correctness, and so its press release tried to conform the results to its dogma. This led to amusing differences between the newspaper reports that merely copied the press release and those written by reporters who paid attention to the data. The data supported the results of independent

polls showing that most Americans think that schools should "teach the controversy" by presenting evidence for and against the official orthodoxy. That was how *New York Times* reporter James Glanz played the story—a headline saying that "Survey Finds Support Is Strong for Teaching 2 Origin Theories." The *Kansas City Star,* whose reporters and editors are at war with the Kansas board of education, headlined the same story "Poll Finds Preference for Teaching Evolution Rather Than Creation."

Chapter 4: Science & Modernist Theology

[1]See generally Edward J. Larson and Larry Witham, "Scientists and Religion in America," *Scientific American,* September 1999, pp. 88-93. The specific years Leuba chose for his testing have a fortuitous significance: 1914 is the year many historians regard as the effective beginning of the twentieth century, when World War I erupted to shatter the nineteenth-century social order and disappoint the progressive optimism of the intellectuals; 1933 was the year that Hitler took power in Germany, Franklin Delano Roosevelt assumed the American presidency, and a group of naive intellectuals led by the philosopher John Dewey published a manifesto of "religious humanism." This manifesto predicted that the expected demise of theistic religion would usher in a new era of scientific progress and social cooperation, permitting the "fullest realization" of mankind's "inherent possibilities." Soon afterward Hitler and Stalin provided a stunning demonstration of some of those inherent possibilities. See my book *Darwin on Trial* (Downers Grove, Ill: InterVarsity Press, 1993), p. 131. I wish a third poll had been taken in 1959, the year of the triumphant centennial celebration of Darwin's *Origin of Species* at the University of Chicago.

[2]"The 1998 NAS members perhaps provide a more immaculate sample of the elite than Leuba's starred entries did. Congress created the National Academy of Sciences in 1863, and after naming its first members Congress empowered them and their successors to choose all later members. Its current membership of 1800 remains the closest thing to a peerage in American science" (Larson and Witham, "Scientists and Religion," p. 90 n. 1).

[3]John Haught, *Science and Religion: From Conflict to Conversation* (Mahwah, N.J.: Paulist, 1995), p. 61.

[4]Ibid., pp. 61-62.

[5]Arthur Peacocke, quoted in an interview in Russell Stannard, *Science and Wonders* (New York: Faber & Faber, 1996), pp. 129-30.

[6]Kenneth R. Miller, *Finding Darwin's God: A Scientist's Search for Common Ground Between God and Evolution* (New York: Cliff Street, 1999), pp. 239-40. In an interview published in the Brown University newspaper, Miller stated that "I believe in God because of evolution. Evolution is how a creator can create a being with absolute free will." Miller's basic logic, common to many theological modernists, is that the discovery of quantum indeterminacy means that future events are not determined by the past or by inviolable laws. What this logic fails to take into account is that actions that are determined by chance are no more freely willed than actions that are determined by law. The Brown interview is found on the Web at <www.browndailyherald.com/stories.cfm?ID=453>.

[7]In his biology textbook Miller makes the preposterous claim that Darwin "remained a devout Christian all his life" (Kenneth R. Miller and Joseph Levine, *Biology,* 5th teachers ed. [Columbus, Ohio: Prentice Hall, 2000], p. 270). On the contrary, Darwin was never more than a lukewarm believer, and by the time of his death described himself as an agnostic. He

was generally reticent on the subject to avoid offending his devout wife or prejudicing the public against his theory, but there is no doubt that he rejected Christianity. He described Christianity as a "damnable doctrine" which if true would require the eternal punishment of his own father and brother, and most of his friends. The Darwin family published a sanitized version of his autobiography, censoring the most vehemently anti-Christian passages but still portraying him as a reluctant agnostic (see James Moore, *The Darwin Legend* [Grand Rapids, Mich.: Baker, 1994], pp. 60-65; and the widely acclaimed biography by Adrian Desmond and James Moore, *Darwin: The Life of a Tormented Evolutionist* [New York: W. W. Norton, 1995], especially pp. 656-58). Flatly contradicting the claim in his textbook, Miller writes that "Darwin in his later years tried and failed to find God, at least a God consistent with his theories." Nonetheless Miller (like John Haught) thinks that biological evolution is necessary to a theology that allows freedom. He reasons that "a biologically static world would leave a Creator's creatures with neither freedom nor the independence required to exercise that freedom. In biological terms, evolution is the only way a Creator could have made us the creatures we are—free beings in a world of authentic and meaningful moral and spiritual choices" (*Finding Darwin's God*, p. 291).

[8]Einstein's famous remark was delivered in 1940 in an address on "Science and Religion" at a conference in New York City (see Max Jammer, *Einstein and Religion* [Princeton, N.J.: Princeton University Press, 1991], p. 31). Einstein explained in this address that there should be no conflict between science and religion because science ascertains only what *is,* not what *should be.* He went on to say that "the main source of the present-day conflicts between the spheres of religion and of science lies in this concept of a personal God" (pp. 94-95).

[9]Ibid., pp. 44-45. Einstein's argument for Spinoza's determinism is immodest, coercive and incoherent. If others fail to appreciate that inviolable laws govern all human thought, feeling and action, then this is because they lack the "unusual integrity, magnanimity and modesty" which enables Einstein himself to see the truth. They must either submit to Einstein and Spinoza or confess to grave character flaws. But if natural laws govern all human thought, then these laws cause both Einstein's belief in determinism and the contrary beliefs of other people. In that case, virtues or flaws have nothing to do with it. We believe or disbelieve as the laws direct and have no choice in the matter.

[10]Kenneth Miller and Joseph Levine, *Biology,* 4th ed. (Columbus, Ohio: Prentice Hall, 1998), sect. 30-32: "In many ways, each animal phylum represents an experiment in the design of body structures to perform the tasks necessary for survival. Of course, there has never been any kind of plan to these experiments because evolution works without either plan or purpose. Nevertheless, the appearance of each phylum in the fossil record represents the random evolutionary development of a basic body plan. . . . It is important to keep in mind that: *Evolution is random and undirected"* (emphasis in original). This is standard evolutionary naturalism, not peculiar in any way to this textbook. As is often the case, the caveat that evolution is undirected has to be repeated and emphasized because otherwise the reference to concepts like "experiments" and even "body plans" would tend to suggest the opposite conclusion. In *Finding Darwin's God* Miller explains: "Evolution is a natural process, and natural processes are undirected. Even if God can intervene in nature, why should he when nature can do a perfectly fine job of achieving His aims all by itself? It was God, after all, who chose the universal constants that make life possible" (p. 244).

[11]Stephen Jay Gould, "Nonoverlapping Magisteria," *Natural History,* March 1997, p. 16.

[12]Pope John Paul II's statement to the Pontifical Academy of Sciences on October 22, 1996, can be found at various sites on the Internet, including <www.cco.caltech.edu/~newman/sci-cp/evolution.html>.

[13]Stephen Jay Gould, *Rocks of Ages: Science and Religion in the Fullness of Life,* Library of Contemporary Thought (Westminster, Md.: Ballantine, 1999), pp. 84-85.

[14]John F. Haught, "The Darwinian Struggle: Catholics, Pay Attention," *Commonwealth,* September 24, 1999, pp. 14, 16. Haught was commenting specifically on an essay Gould had written for *Time* (August 23, 1999) rather than on Gould's NOMA essay or his book *Rocks of Ages.* The Darwinian philosopher of science Michael Ruse was ever more severe in his criticism. He wrote that "Gould certainly does think that science and religion clash. Claims, for instance, about walking on water or multiplying loaves and fishes or rising on the third day are simply false. Which means, according to Gould's agenda, that they must be eliminated from religion, so that the clashes are removed. It is like someone insisting that a size ten shoe does in fact fit all sizes, and by ensuring that it does by putting in packing for small feet and cutting off the ends for large feet. In this sense, frankly, Gould is being a bit of a phoney and it is no wonder that people are irritated. . . . What I am saying is that Gould should not pretend to one and really opt for the other. He is hunting with the atheists and running with the believers. That is bad faith, in the language of the existentialists. You may not care much for Dawkins and his arguments, but at least he is open and honest, and that is no small thing" (Michael Ruse, "Being Mean to Steve," on "Metaviews," <www.meta-list.org>).

[15]Richard Dawkins, "Snake Oil and Holy Water: Illogical Thinking Is the Only Thing Joining Science and Religion Together," *Forbes ASAP,* October 4, 1999, pp. 235-38; also found at <www.forbes.com/asap/99/1004/235.htm>.

[16]Ibid.

Chapter 5: Darwinism of the Mind

[1]Richard Dawkins, *The Selfish Gene* (Oxford: Oxford University Press 1976), pp. v.

[2]Charles Darwin, *The Descent of Man* (Princeton, N.J.: Princeton University Press, 1981), p. 201: "At some future period, not very distant as measured by centuries, the civilized races of man will almost certainly exterminate and replace throughout the world the savage races."

[3]Dawkins, *Selfish Gene,* p. 3.

[4]The Dawkins-Pinker exchange is available at <www.edge.org/documents/archive/edge53.html>.

[5]The quotation is from the summary at <www.newscientist.com/ns/19990313/mememyself.html>.

[6]Michael Kelly, "Arguing for Infanticide," *Washington Post,* November 6, 1997.

[7]Steven Pinker, "Arguing Against Infanticide," *Washington Post,* November 21, 1997.

[8]Steven Pinker, *How the Mind Works* (New York: W. W. Norton, 1997), pp. 55-56.

[9]Andrew Ferguson, "How Steven Pinker's Mind Works," *The Weekly Standard,* January 12, 1998, p. 16.

[10]See Pinker, *How the Mind Works,* n. 7.

[11]Steven Pinker, "A Matter of the Soul," *The Weekly Standard,* February 2, 1998.

[12]John Searle, *Mind, Language, and Society: Philosophy in the Real World* (New York: Basic-Books, 1998). This slim volume succinctly summarizes views that Searle has advocated over

the years in many books and articles.

¹³Paul M. Churchland and Patricia S. Churchland, *On the Contrary: Critical Essays, 1987-1997* (Cambridge, Mass.: Bradford/MIT Press, 1998). Patricia Churchland authored some of the essays in this volume and shares the general views of her husband, so the two are often cited as "the Churchlands." The Churchland and Searle views are insightfully described and contrasted in a review essay by Colin McGinn in *The New York Review of Books*, June 10, 1999, titled "Can We Ever Understand Consciousness?" This essay is available on the Internet at <www.nybooks.com/nyrev/WWWarchdisplay.cgi?19990610044R>.

¹⁴Searle, *Mind, Language, and Society*, p. 51.

¹⁵John Horgan, *The Undiscovered Mind: How the Human Brain Defies Replication, Medication, and Explanation* (New York: Free Press, 1999).

¹⁶Quoted in ibid., p. 229.

¹⁷Ibid., pp. 258-59.

¹⁸Edward O. Wilson, *Consilience: The Unity of Knowledge* (New York: Knopf, 1998). Wilson summarizes his thesis on p. 266: "The Central Idea of the consilience world view is that all tangible phenomena, from the birth of stars to the workings of social institutions, are based on material processes that are ultimately reducible, however long and tortuous the sequences, to the laws of physics."

Chapter 6: The Empire Strikes Back

¹Richard Dawkins, *The Blind Watchmaker* (New York: W. W. Norton, 1996), pp. 2-3.

²Darwin himself insisted that a theory of historical descent without an adequate mechanism would be unsatisfactory. He wrote in the introduction to *The Origin of Species* that "in considering the Origin of Species, it is quite conceivable that a naturalist, reflecting on the mutual affinities of organic beings, on their embryological relations, their geographical distribution, geological succession, and such other facts, might come to the conclusion that each species had not been independently created, but had descended, like varieties, from other species. Nevertheless, such a conclusion, even if well founded, would be unsatisfactory, until it could be shown how the innumerable species inhabiting this world have been modified, so as to acquire that perfection of structure and coadaptation which most justly excites our admiration" (Charles Darwin, *The Origin of Species*, Norton critical ed. [New York: W. W. Norton, 1979], p. 36).

³The terms *naturalism, materialism* and *physicalism* are all equivalent for present purposes and may be used interchangeably.

⁴Kenneth R. Miller, *Finding Darwin's God: A Scientist's Search for Common Ground Between God and Evolution* (New York: HarperCollins 1999), pp. 27-28.

⁵Ibid., p. 93. The most frequently cited example of evolutionary speciation is the thirteen or so species of finches on the various islands of the Galapagos chain. In this case the question is not whether the finches all descended from a single ancestral type but whether they are truly separate species—since they can interbreed when given the opportunity.

⁶Ibid., pp. 94-99. Although the elephant case is Miller's prime example, he also refers to various other examples that are said to illustrate possible macroevolutionary transitions in the vertebrate sequence—e.g., from fish to amphibian. As I have pointed out in various books and articles, Darwinists do not test their theory against the fossil record as a whole but mine the record selectively for confirming examples—meaning examples of fossils that suggest a

possible evolutionary sequence to the eye of a believer. There is no objective standard for telling the difference between fossils that merely resemble each other in some respects and those in a genuine ancestor-descendant relationship. I will not develop this critique further here because I dealt with the subject in chapters 4-6 of *Darwin on Trial* and because arguments over fossil stories tend to distract attention from Darwinism's crucial weakness. Even if there is a record of continuity of succession, which is very doubtful if all the evidence is considered without prejudice, this pattern provides us with no information about the source of complex genetic information.

[7]Miller, *Finding Darwin's God,* p. 126.

[8]Ibid., p. 217.

[9]Robert Pennock, *Tower of Babel: The Evidence Against the New Creationism* (Cambridge, Mass.: Bradford Books, 1999), p. 203.

[10]Pennock says that linguists disagree about whether there are separate language "trees" or only one, but settles the matter with the comment that "most linguists accept the single source thesis as a working hypothesis, if only for the sake of simplicity" (Pennock, *Tower of Babel,* p. 144). An assumption of that kind has no evidentiary value, but I accept it *arguendo* for present purposes.

[11]Steven Pinker, *The Language Instinct* (New York: Harper, 1994), pp. 238-39.

[12]Ibid., p. 238.

[13]Ibid., p. 27.

[14]Ibid., p. 355. Pinker takes the more typical Darwinian view that the more complex an adaptive capacity seems to be, the more necessary it is to attribute its origin to natural selection. As Pinker puts it, "Natural selection is not just a scientifically respectable alternative to divine creation. It is the *only* alternative that can explain the evolution of a complex organ like the eye. The reason that the choice is so stark—God or natural selection—is that structures that can do what the eye does are extremely low-probability arrangements" (pp. 360-61). One meets that argument over and over again in the Darwinist literature. Even the most speculative just-so story, ungrounded in any testable process or fossil evidence, is preferable to allowing God a role or invoking design. Darwinian explanations that rest on little more than that reasoning then become established fact in the Darwinian mind and hence evidence for the truth of the theory.

[15]For further detail on the controversies among the Darwinists, see chapter four of Phillip Johnson, *Reason in the Balance* (Downers Grove, Ill.: InterVarsity Press, 1995), and also the essays "The Unraveling of Scientific Materialism" and "The Gorbachev of Darwinism" in my *Objections Sustained* (Downers Grove, Ill.: InterVarsity Press, 1998). These quotations from Maynard Smith, Lewontin and Gould in this paragraph are from essays available at the *New York Review of Books* Web site: <www.nybooks.com/nyrev>.

Chapter 7: Building a New Foundation for Reason

[1]J. I. Packer, *Knowing God* (Downers Grove, Ill.: InterVarsity Press, 1993), pp. 11-12. Packer credits the balcony metaphor to theologian John Mackay.

[2]Richard Dickerson, essay published in *Journal of Molecular Evolution* 34 (1992): 277; and *Perspectives in Science and Christian Faith* 44 (1991): 137-38. Quoted by Michael Behe, *Darwin's Black Box: The Biochemical Challenge to Evolution* (New York: Free Press, 1996), pp. 238-39.

[3]For details on the Cambrian explosion, peppered moth story, Haeckel embryo drawings and other evidence discrediting Darwinian claims, see Jonathan Wells, *Icons of Evolution* (Washington, D.C.: Regnery, 2000).

[4]I vividly remember my experience at a scientific conference in Varenna, Italy, in September 1998, where I presented a paper explaining the "two definitions of science" thesis. The paper is on the Internet at <www.arn.org/docs/johnson/scirel98.htm>. Immediately after my lecture, the famous origin-of-life biochemist Christian de Duve sternly admonished me, both in the public questioning period and privately at lunch, that I was "attacking science." De Duve has so much natural courtesy that even his rebukes are a pleasure to receive. I cannot be as admiring of his logic, however, because he tried to say all at once that (1) science is not committed to any philosophy and (2) to question materialism or naturalism is to repudiate science. He did not think he was contradicting himself because he took for granted that reason and naturalism are the same thing.

[5]See J. Budziszewski, *The Revenge of Conscience* (Dallas, Tex.: Spence, 1999).

[6]Richard Dawkins, *The Blind Watchmaker* (New York: W. W. Norton, 1996), p. 1.

[7]Francis Crick, *What Mad Pursuit* (New York: BasicBooks, 1988), p. 138.

[8]The questions "Who do men say that I am?" and "Who do *you* say that I am?" are recorded in Matthew 16:13-16, Mark 8:27-29 and Luke 9:18-20.

[9]Freeman Dyson, "Is God in the Lab?" *New York Review of Books,* May 28, 1998; also found at <www.nybooks.com/nyrev/WWWarchdisplay.cgi?19980528008R>. Dyson was reviewing two books: John Polkinghorne's *Belief in God in an Age of Science* (New Haven, Conn.: Yale University Press, 1998); and Richard Feynman's *The Meaning of It All: Thoughts of a Citizen Scientist* (Reading, Mass.: Addison Wesley, 1999). In my opinion Polkinghorne's title invites the kind of dismissal Dyson gave it. In an "age of science" God has at most a tenuous cognitive standing. If we do our best to think about the same subject from God's point of view, we might frame the question as the proper limits of science within the governance of God. Very few elite scientists can even conceive of thinking about the question that way.

Chapter 8: Technological Optimism & Literary Despair

[1]John Searle, *Mind, Language, and Society* (New York:BasicBooks, 1998), p. 35.

[2]That assumption is provisional. If Christians have nothing to say that they can defend in public on the highest intellectual standards, then it is doubtful whether what they say in private is more substantial than quackery.

[3]Lesslie Newbigin, *Truth to Tell: The Gospel as Public Truth* (Grand Rapids, Mich.: Eerdmans, 1991), p. 24. Newbigin credits the Chinese scholar Carver Yu with inventing the phrase "technological optimism and literary despair" but provides no citation.

[4]Alvin Kernan, *In Plato's Cave* (New Haven, Conn.: Yale University Press, 1999).

[5]According to the eminent military historian John Keegan's *The Battle for History: Re-Fighting World War II* (New York: Random House, 1995): "Wars are won by good leaders but fought by their brave and often anonymous underlings. The Second World War has yielded a plethora of personal memoirs of the war experience at the small-unit and individual level. . . . A third memoir of the [Pacific Theater] action, also late to appear, which seems destined to become a classic, is Alvin Kernan's *Crossing the Line* (Annapolis, Md.: U.S. Naval Institute Press, 1997). Kernan was a poor Wyoming boy, a child of the Depression, who enlisted as an ordinary seaman to escape a life without prospects in a rural backwater. Chance placed him

aboard an aircraft carrier in the Pacific before Pearl Harbor, and there consigned him to fly as an enlisted aircrewman in fighters and strike aircraft during the great air-sea battles of the war, from Midway to Okinawa. He survived the sinking of his first carrier, a ditching off another, and a series of aerial combats, for one of which he was awarded the Navy Cross. *Crossing the Line* is an extraordinary book, most of all for the sense it conveys of the isolation of the individual in an enormous, impersonal organization into which nevertheless, danger might at any instant intrude with an acutely personal immediacy" (pp. 62-64).

[6]Kernan, *Crossing the Line*, p. 2.

[7]Ibid., p. 274.

[8]Ibid., p. 272.

[9]Ibid., p. 67.

[10]Lesslie Newbigin, *Truth to Tell: The Gospel as Public Truth* (Grand Rapids, Mich.: Eerdmans, 1991), p. 26. Newbigin adds this significant comment: "In a sense—and I hope not over dramatizing—one could say that the new Cartesian starting point, which has been so foundational for all that has followed, was a small-scale repetition of the Fall. Adam is not content to trust God. He wants to have his own certitude, based on an experimental test of the validity of God's promise. He is the first inductive theologian" (p. 27). Throughout his writings Newbigin credits the influence of Michael Polanyi, especially from Polanyi's dense masterwork *Personal Knowledge* (Chicago: University of Chicago Press, 1974).

Index

For more information on Phillip Johnson, intelligent design, materialist philosophy and empirical science, or to view a presentation on Darwinism by Phillip Johnson, visit our website at <www.wedgeoftruth.com>.